PRAISE FOR
VERTICAL MARRIAGE

If your marriage isn't vertical, then it's just a matter of time before your relationship will pay the price. Or . . . you could read this book and transform your marriage into a page-turning, smoking-hot, this-is-more-like-it love story. Your call.

DR. TIM KIMMEL, author of *Grace Filled Marriage*

We athletes invest countless hours of time and money into giving ourselves the greatest chance of not just success but greatness. Taking the time to read this book will do for your marriage what all great athletes do for their careers—find the people who are the absolute best at what they do and allow them to pour into every part of you as an athlete. This book will radically change you as a person and a partner, and, like Tiffany and me, you'll become a part of a marriage that thrives because of these teachings and principles. If you want your marriage to be different, *Vertical Marriage* by Dave and Ann Wilson is the difference maker.

DAN AND TIFFANY ORLOVSKY, twelve-year
NFL quarterback and seven-year member of
the Detroit Lions (Dan and Tiffany have the
honor of having been married by Dave)

I think what I love most about my friends Dave and Ann Wilson is their honesty, coupled with their passion for couples to experience marriage as God intends it. Wherever you are in your relationship, *Vertical Marriage* will move you closer together as you learn how to go vertical together.

BOB LEPINE, cohost of *FamilyLife Today*

Vertical Marriage will provide a virtually life-changing message for all couples seeking God's presence in their marriage. It's a very entertaining read packed with real-life experiences that all married couples can relate to. Dave and Ann Wilson provide dual perspectives that blend seamlessly into the singular concept of a vertical marriage.

JIM CALDWELL, seven-year NFL head coach
and two-time Super Bowl champion

Dave and Ann Wilson have a unique ability to authentically reveal their scars, glorifying God as the centerpiece throughout the process. Their impact on our marriage is immeasurable, and we are eternally grateful for both of them.

DREW AND KRISTIN STANTON,
Cleveland Browns quarterback

One of the reasons I have a healthy marriage today is because of how Pastor Dave and Ann Wilson poured into me as a teenager. As someone who spent my high school years in their church, they modeled an authentic and persevering marriage centered on Christ. Dave and Ann are transparent, wise, and relatable. You will get to be a "fly on the wall" as they share their stories and hard-won insight. *Vertical Marriage* is not about trying harder; it's about trying again. I'm so glad they tried again and again. Our marriage shapes future generations. Let this book encourage you, no matter what season you're in.

ESTHER FLEECE ALLEN, speaker and
author of *No More Faking Fine*

It's rare to have a great marriage. It's rare to be a great communicator. Put those things together, and you have the right book for the right person from the right authors. I'm a fan of Dave and Ann Wilson and *Vertical Marriage*. They have helped me, and they will help you too.

BRIAN TOME, senior pastor of Crossroads
Church, Cincinnati, Ohio

My favorite marriage speakers finally wrote a book—one I've been asking them to write since I first heard them speak on stage almost ten years ago. The Wilsons are the real deal, and reading *Vertical Marriage* gives us a peek into their life and marriage, but not in a stuffy Christian way where you listen to some pastor who doesn't really let you into their real world. This book isn't like others that seem far from obtainable. You'll get practical advice and wisdom from a couple who has gone the distance and are willing to help you learn from their mistakes so you don't make them. This book will encourage you and may even leave you feeling good about where you're at in your marriage, not just overwhelm you with depressing news and more work to do.

CRAIG GROSS, founder of XXXchurch.com

Dave and Ann Wilson are amazing at breaking down how and why to do marriage right. Not only is the information in *Vertical Marriage* legit, but it works. They know how to make it fun. I'm also amazed that Dave finally sat still long enough to write it all down!

MICHAEL JR, comedian and author of *The Parts We Play*

Dave and Ann Wilson have been gifted by God to speak into the hearts of marriages across this country. We've been blessed to sit under and learn relationship principles from the Wilsons for three years, and we still seek their counsel today. What a blessing *Vertical Marriage* will be to countless couples who will experience in print what so many have experienced in person through their church, their speaking ministry, and their ministry as chaplains for the Detroit Lions for more than thirty years. Their transparency, commitment to biblical marriage, and pertinent stories will convict, challenge, and encourage everyone who reads this book.

JON AND JEN KITNA, seventeen-year NFL quarterback and current high school head football coach

As a professional athlete, I utilize experts in every facet of my career to be the best. Striving to be the best, of course, doesn't stop on the field. Elise and I want the most fulfilling marriage we can have, and *Vertical Marriage*, written by two relationship experts, shows us how to have it by striving to be vertically aligned with Christ. Elise and I trust Dave and Ann Wilson as true experts and mentors—as a couple who has been through it all.

GOLDEN AND ELISE TATE, Detroit Lions
receiver and Super Bowl champion

I had an idea that I could transform my husband into the man I wanted him to be. By the grace of God, Dave and Ann Wilson came into my life. I came to see that my husband didn't need to be fixed; my own personal view did. With their guidance I was able to refocus, and fifteen years later, we're still putting the Do Not Disturb sign on the door every night!

KOREN FURREY, wife of the hottest NFL
coach around—Mike Furrey ☺

VERTICAL

Marriage

VERTICAL

Marriage

THE ONE SECRET THAT WILL
CHANGE YOUR MARRIAGE

DAVE AND ANN WILSON
WITH JOHN DRIVER

ZONDERVAN
BOOKS

ZONDERVAN BOOKS

Vertical Marriage
Copyright © 2019 by Dave and Ann Wilson

Requests for information should be addressed to:
Zondervan, *3900 Sparks Drive SE, Grand Rapids, Michigan 49546*

Zondervan titles may be purchased in bulk for educational, business, fundraising, or sales promotional use. For information, please email SpecialMarkets@Zondervan.com.

ISBN 978-0-310-36204-3 (softcover)
ISBN 978-0-310-35683-7 (audio)

The Library of Congress has cataloged the hardcover edition as follows:

Names: Wilson, Dave, 1957 October 15- author. | Wilson, Ann, 1960- author. | Driver, John, 1978- author.
Title: Vertical marriage : the one secret that will change your marriage / Dave and Ann Wilson, with John Driver.
Description: Grand Rapids, MI : Zondervan, [2019]
Identifiers: LCCN 2018020255| ISBN 9780310352143 (hardcover) | ISBN 9780310352174 (epub)
Subjects: LCSH: Marriage--Religious aspects--Christianity.
Classification: LCC BV835 .W56475 2019 | DDC 248.8/44--dc23 LC record available at https://lccn.loc.gov/2018020255

All Scripture quotations, unless otherwise indicated, are taken from The Holy Bible, New International Version®, NIV®. Copyright © 1973, 1978, 1984, 2011 by Biblica, Inc.® Used by permission of Zondervan. All rights reserved worldwide. www.Zondervan.com. The "NIV" and "New International Version" are trademarks registered in the United States Patent and Trademark Office by Biblica, Inc.® • Scripture quotations marked AMP are taken from the Amplified® Bible. Copyright © 1954, 1958, 1962, 1964, 1965, 1987, 2015 by The Lockman Foundation. Used by permission. (www.Lockman.org). • Scripture quotations marked ESV are taken from the ESV® Bible (The Holy Bible, English Standard Version®). Copyright © 2001 by Crossway, a publishing ministry of Good News Publishers. Used by permission. All rights reserved. • Scripture quotations marked NASB are taken from the New American Standard Bible®. Copyright © 1960, 1962, 1963, 1968, 1971, 1972, 1973, 1975, 1977, 1995 by The Lockman Foundation. Used by permission. (www.Lockman.org). • Scripture quotations marked TLB are taken from The Living Bible. Copyright © 1971. Used by permission of Tyndale House Publishers, Inc., Carol Stream, Illinois 60188. All rights reserved.

Any internet addresses (websites, blogs, etc.) and telephone numbers in this book are offered as a resource. They are not intended in any way to be or imply an endorsement by Zondervan, nor does Zondervan vouch for the content of these sites and numbers for the life of this book.

Published in association with the literary agency of Wolgemuth & Associates, Inc.

Cover design: James W. Hall IV
Cover illustrations: wundervisuals / Getty Images
Interior design: Kait Lamphere

Printed in the United States of America

---

22 23 24 25 26 27 28 29 30 /LSC/ 15 14 13 12 11 10 9 8 7

At the foot of our wedding bed, we knelt and prayed
that God would grant us a legacy
that would impact the world for his kingdom.
God is answering that prayer
through our three sons and their wives,
to whom we dedicate this book.

CJ and Robin: you bring the grace and joy of Jesus
to everyone you encounter.
Austin and Kendall: you carry the heart
of Christ everywhere you go
and are pouring that into your sweet kids—
Olive, Porter, and Holden.
Cody and Jenna: your passion and
surrender to Jesus are compelling
and will transform generations to come.
Lead on!

May our legacy point Vertical First
for generations to come!

CONTENTS

PART THREE:
Intimacy

PART FOUR:
Living Vertical

FOREWORD

When God created Dave Wilson and Ann Baron, he had big plans in mind!

When God called them to become Dave and Ann Wilson, God smiled as he watched them embrace his plan.

And when Dave and Ann surrendered their lives and marriage on their tenth anniversary, God showed up and changed the trajectory of their lives so that they've been able to impact hundreds of thousands of other lives.

Barbara and I have known Dave and Ann for more than three decades. We've watched them excel as individuals, as a couple, and as a family. They have spoken at more than one hundred FamilyLife Weekend to Remember marriage getaways to tens of thousands of couples. They are very good friends and trusted emissaries in bringing help and hope to marriages and families.

You are about to profoundly benefit from "The Secret" that is shared in this book by two of our favorite people.

Your funny bone is about to get a workout. The Wilsons are not only a winsome and authentic couple, but they are incurably funny, entertaining, and compellingly fresh in their communication to this generation.

Your heart is about to be massaged and strengthened as they give you and your spouse courage to go the distance in your marriage. They will stimulate your heart to keep on risking the ingredients of a great marriage—humility, love, and forgiveness.

Your life is about to be transformed as you are challenged to reject the ruts of complacency and mediocrity in your marriage and press forward together with lives that experience the ultimate adventure of following Jesus. Dave and Ann are on a mission, and they want you to personally know what it's like to see God use you to model his love for others to see.

You've not only made a great choice to pick up this book; you've made a brave choice. Fasten your seat belt—the ride will be exhilarating and challenging, and we predict this will be one of the very best investments in your marriage and family you could ever make.

Dennis and Barbara Rainey
cofounders of FamilyLife and
hosts of *FamilyLife Today*

PART ONE

Going Vertical

One

SIX WORDS
That Changed Everything

A life—a marriage—is built on moments. They are the small and seemingly insignificant bricks that, stacked one by one over time, quietly ascend upon themselves into giant walls, breathtaking columns, and bridges over all kinds of waters. Our lives are built brick by brick. Moment by moment. Many of these moments fly by and, to be quite honest, are not really *that* memorable. After all, they are just little bricks.

But every once in a while, one of those "little" bricks breaks loose from the wall of life, careening toward you like a ton of . . . well, you know. That little masonry moment looks you right in the eye as if to say, "Listen up, dude! What you choose in the next five minutes will determine the rest of your life—and even your kids' lives!"

I (Dave) experienced one of those "pay attention to the brick" moments in the tenth year of my marriage.

Pause.

Introductions

Before we get to that story, we should probably get acquainted first—both with each other and with the journey we are about to take together. My name is Dave, and this is my wife, Ann.

Say hi, Ann.

Hello! Ann here. Yes, I know this is an unorthodox introduction, switching voices between paragraphs and whatnot, but you should probably get used to the unorthodox. More on that to come.

For now, though, I just want to introduce myself and let you know that in addition to Dave, I'm also wrapped up in these words that fill the pages in front of you. But what you are experiencing right now is what will periodically happen throughout this book: Dave and I will sometimes share stories and insights as individuals, and then sometimes we will decide to jump in together and speak as "us"—a perhaps predictable, yet perfect metaphor for "two" becoming "one" in marriage.

In fact, just for practice, watch as Dave and I magically morph into "us" in the next paragraph in three . . . two . . . one . . .

When Two Become One

And here we are. Us. The transition was painless, yes? Good. We only wish that the melding of two lives together in marriage was also painless. Maybe you thought it was going to be. And maybe from whatever stage of marriage you are in, from newlywed to seasoned veteran, it still feels fairly painless.

Maybe.

But the odds are that if you fall into any chronological category beyond the first two weeks of marriage, your married life probably doesn't feel exactly painless. This doesn't necessarily mean your marriage is in crisis; it just means your marriage is real.

Maybe you don't yet have a seamless "us" voice because you don't yet know how "us" is supposed to work. Maybe you feel that *you* are somehow being lost in the mix. Not sure what to let go of and what to cling to. Not sure which comments to let pass by and which ones to freak out about. Or maybe your "us" is going really well, but you still want to keep growing in it.

Maybe at this point, you have lost all hope for your marriage. If you're being honest, you might admit that you can't even get your spouse to look at this book with you. Perhaps you're struggling to even hold on for another day. For you, we just want to tell you that no matter where you are, though it may be hard for you to believe, we get it . . . we've been there.

And because we've been there, we want to ask you to do something that may feel impossible. Just for this moment right now, instead of giving up, will you hang in there a little longer? And while you hold on for dear life, will you be willing to ask God to work on *you*? Yes, *just you*.

Let's be honest, you've probably already discovered that you can't change your spouse anyway. It feels like a horrible realization, but trust us—this realization is true for all of us, and discovering it is actually a very good thing, even though it hurts at first. So for now, will you be willing to let God work on *just you*?

In our marriage, both of us were pretty messed up in our own ways, even though we thought it was the other's fault. We'll tell you the full story later, but just know that within the first six months of our marriage, one of us looked at the other and said, "I wish I would have never married you!"

Ouch.

So yeah, we get how it feels to live in hopelessness about your marriage. But regardless of the scenario you find yourself in, we have news for you: even though we are still married today, we don't have everything about marriage figured out. Not in the least. But now that you know this, we can also tell you that this is actually good news . . . really, really good news. Why?

Because our mission is *not* to fix you or your marriage. Fixing is something you do to broken pottery or leaky car engines. Our mission is to share a secret with you that will completely revolutionize both your personal life and your marriage in a way no amount of human wit or wisdom can even begin to offer.

That's a pretty big promise, right?

Indeed, but we boldly make it because our confidence doesn't lie in what we know on our own, but rather in something that has been continually revealed to us over the years. As our culture tears marriages and families apart, it is apparent that we are not equipped with the tools or knowledge for making our marriages healthy and lasting. Most of us end up just getting by, settling for so much less than the life we dreamed of . . . that *God* dreams of for us.

So we *don't* aim to fix you, but we *do* aim to both show and tell you how we are deeply flawed, just like the rest of us. We promise to be honest—even painfully so—as we point out some of the things that have been pointed out to us along the way. Through our own personal narrative of matrimonial highs and lows, we plan to share the elusive secret to finding the joy and the relational transformation God has so graciously designed each of us to experience.

Trust me, this is a secret that no one seems to know. We have talked with thousands of couples over the years at our marriage conferences, and virtually no one seems to know the most important truth that can transform their marriage. We didn't know it either! Sneak preview: the secret to a great marriage is to *go vertical*, inviting God into your worst conflicts and unsolvable dilemmas.

Many times, we will alternate chapters between the two of us, but at times (and we'll give you plenty of warning), we will come back and speak together as "us." Why? So that no matter who you are, you can experience both a male and a female perspective of the challenges and adventures we all face in marriage . . . and through the big secret of vertical marriage, we hope that you will also develop into the kind of "us" that God intends for your marriage.

We look forward to the journey with you, but for now, let's get back to our regularly scheduled Dave, who was about to tell you a story about a memorable date . . .

Our Tenth Anniversary

I (Dave) thought our tenth wedding anniversary would be one of the greatest nights of my life—actually, of *our* lives. By that time, Ann and I had built an incredible life together. We tied the knot in Ohio and then moved to the University of Nebraska, where in 1980 I became the chaplain for the Cornhuskers varsity sports teams. After two years there, we decided to pursue more training for a life of ministry together. So we headed west to California to attend seminary.

Three years later, I had a master of divinity, and, more importantly, Ann was pregnant with our first son. We moved to Detroit, where I was blessed not only with two more sons, but also with the opportunity to become the youngest chaplain in the NFL—with the Detroit Lions. There I also met Steve Andrews, and we began dreaming of starting a church together. It seemed at the time that life could not be better.

What could go wrong?

Fast-forward to May 24, 1990. It was our tenth anniversary, and I had planned this night for months. The ten-year mark is obviously a big deal, so I decided to go all out. This meant securing a reservation at an *upscale* restaurant in an *upscale* part of Detroit—and all at an *upscale* price. By this time, we had two healthy and happy sons. But tonight, it was just the two of us, and I knew it was going to be an unforgettable evening.

Spending big money on a date is a big deal for me, as I'm pretty much known as a tightwad, since I really do like my cash to be kept in a nice, tight wad—never to be opened! A buddy of mine says it would take the Jaws of Life to pry open my wallet. But on this night, those jaws came unhinged, and I spent a little bit—no, actually a whole wad—of cash.

I wanted Ann to be reminded that marrying me was the best decision of her life.

When Friday night finally arrived, we donned our best clothes and headed out to the restaurant. I worked out an agreement with our waiter to have ten roses brought to our table at strategic times throughout the dinner. Each rose represented a year of our marriage. So after we settled in and ordered some hors d'oeuvres, I gave the waiter a "look," and he placed rose number one on the tablecloth. We then shared memories of our first year of marriage.

I could immediately tell that I was *killing it* in the romance department with Ann. She seemed so excited to "taaalk" about our relationship. Every guy knows that women don't just talk. Men talk, but women like to "taaalk"—sharing details, feelings, and anything else that we men would rarely share voluntarily. Well, on this night, we were "taaalking," and Ann was loving it. And if Ann was loving it, then that meant I was scoring points. Major points that would no doubt pay off later, if you know what I mean.

After ten minutes or so of reminiscing about year one, I gave the waiter the "look" again, and he brought over the second rose. I knew I was giving this college-aged kid a real lesson in how to woo a woman. Heck, I all but expected him to leave *me* a tip later on.

The dinner couldn't have gone any better. We revisited the high points of each and every one of our ten years together— and all during the course of an amazing meal. After dinner, I had planned another surprise.

Since we were about to embark on the dream of a lifetime by helping to start a church that would kick off in just a few months, I took us to the parking lot of the middle school where our church would soon begin meeting. Ann hadn't yet seen this property, so I thought it might be cool to park in this lot and pray together that God would perform a miracle right there in that location—that he would turn a public middle school into a vibrant church.

But to be completely honest, parking to pray wasn't the only item on my agenda. I also thought it would be pretty sweet if we could just "park"—if you know what I mean. And I was sure that Ann would agree.

It was probably one of the shortest prayer times I had ever led. After the "amen," it was time for the much-anticipated, extracurricular portion of our evening. After all, this date had indeed had all the markings of what every woman longs for:

1. We had gazed into each other's eyes . . .
2. over an amazing meal . . .
3. at a high-end restaurant . . .
4. with romantic discussions and much "taaalking" . . .
5. about how wonderful our marriage has been.

What could possibly go wrong?

When I leaned in to kiss Ann, she turned her head away from me. At first, I assumed that somehow she had innocently failed to recognize that I was making my move. So I tried again. But this time, it became clear she was avoiding my kiss. I was perplexed—so much so that I did what every man hates to do, asking her the question every man hates to ask: "Is anything wrong?"

"No," she replied.

Hmm. After ten years of marriage, I had learned a thing or two about how to read her nonverbal signals. She was saying nothing was wrong, yet her tone and posture were saying something totally different. So I took a deep breath and asked again.

"It seems like you don't want to kiss me. Are you sure nothing's wrong?"

Her stare was alarmingly empty. After a long pause, she finally muttered, "Well, actually there *is* something wrong . . ."

I waited in complete silence. I thought I was doing pretty well as a husband and a dad. I mean, I preached about this stuff. I knew what the Bible says about marriage. I wasn't perfect, but I thought I was practicing what I preached. We'd had a great marriage that I would put up against anybody's. In fact, if you would have asked me to rate my marriage on a scale of one to ten, I would have said it was a ten . . . and if not a ten, a 9.8. And the craziest part is that I would have guaranteed you my wife would agree.

I did not know it right then, but a moment that would forever change our lives was staring us right in the face. Ann said these unforgettable words—the brick I never saw coming.

"Well, to be completely honest, I've lost my feelings for you."

Two

"I'VE LOST MY
Feelings for You"

When I was a teenager, I dreamed of finding, falling for, and then forever cherishing the perfect mate. So when I met Dave Wilson, I felt confident that all my dreams would come true. Actually, let me rephrase that—I had known Dave for years. The first time we spoke to each other, I thought he was the most conceited, arrogant guy I had ever encountered. He seemed to be the furthest thing from the man of my dreams!

You see, back in our hometown, Dave was "the man." He was the local high school All-State quarterback, point guard, and shortstop with good looks, flowing locks, and a dynamic personality—which all went straight to his head. My dad coached him in high school, and I was *not* going to be one of the many girls who fell for his charming ways.

Although he *was* awfully cute.

After Dave went off to college on a football scholarship, I basically lost touch with him. Our only connection came via the newspaper articles I periodically read about his success on the football field. But then during my senior year of high school, I bumped into him when he was home on winter break.

There were rumors that Dave had recently become a Christian at college, but I honestly didn't believe any of them. Back home, Dave was still known as a partier and a womanizer who usually got whatever he wanted. So when I saw him shooting baskets in our high school gym, I walked right up to him and said, "So I hear you've become a Christian?" My smirk and tone made it obvious I didn't believe a word of it.

As Dave answered me, I sensed he was a completely different person. The cockiness and self-centeredness were gone. After only a short time of following Jesus, the change in him was nothing less than remarkable. I didn't see *that* coming. His relationship with Jesus was both real and contagious—and I was quickly drawn to him.

It wasn't long before I broke up with my boyfriend (something that Dave is still proud of) and started dating Dave. This was the first dating relationship that either of us had ever had in which Jesus was the foundation. He made all the difference in the world. With every other guy, I was always stressed about where the relationship was headed. But with Jesus at the center, the stress and anxiety were gone. Christ was in control, and I knew he could be trusted to lead us.

Dave and I fell madly in love with each other—and with Jesus at the same time. Every other dating relationship pulled me away from Jesus, but this one drew me closer. So when I was engaged, the very thought of walking down the aisle to exchange vows with *the* Dave Wilson was literally the most exciting thing I could imagine. My youthful anticipation was like a movie projector in my head, brightly flashing euphoric images onto the screen of my mind. I could only imagine what Dave was going to be like as a husband; after all, he was the godliest man I had ever met. I just knew he was going to lead me spiritually—not to mention he was the hottest guy around.

Jackpot.

I floated on a cloud of blissfulness—a cloud I thought would last forever. One of the most exciting parts of the whole idyllic expectation was what we planned to do together in ministry. We had this vision—a desire for God to do something incredible through us. So not long after our marriage began, this ministry dream also started to become a reality.

But have you ever been in a movie theater when the projector suddenly malfunctions? For me, when the film of my expectations for marriage began to melt, so did my whole world.

The blissful cloud I had floated on had turned into a dense and unyielding fog—and I couldn't escape it. And as we took on more and more, our marriage seemed to become less and less. This was no longer a dream; this was reality, and it was becoming an increasingly difficult reality. The dream that was coming true was not the one I had envisioned.

What I thought would be delightful milestones we would stroll past together in stride instead turned out to be piles of ugly old bricks blocking our pathway forward. Dave said he didn't see one of those bricks coming toward him when it fell off the wall, but I was no stranger to them. Somewhere along the way, I began picking them up one by one until they filled the impossible-to-carry knapsack I dragged behind me daily.

"Are You Leaving *Again*?"

At the time, Dave was working two or three jobs. He was trying so hard—trying to be a dad, a husband, and a church planter. He was leading Bible studies left and right. These were all *good* things that I supported—what sort of person wouldn't? And when the Detroit Lions chaplaincy came about, neither of us could doubt that it was a *great* opportunity for him.

But an NFL season does not make for a smooth family calendar. When he wasn't meeting with players and their families or leading devotionals, he was on the road with the team. He was gone more and more . . . and we were talking less and less. Not to mention that we had two little boys at home who needed him.

And *I* needed him.

I would say things like, "Honey, you've got to be here. The boys are growing up. I need you. The boys need you. I'm longing to spend time with you."

"I know," he would say. But after a while, I questioned whether he really knew. I knew he had every good intention of following through on his every good intention, but there was no way he could do it all. Just when I would think he had put his family first for even one night, he would walk out the door.

"Wait, you're leaving again tonight?"

"Yeah, I got this meeting, and I have to go there to speak to these people."

This conversation happened a thousand times. Night after night of these kinds of exchanges turned into months—and months turned into years.

"Whatever, Dave. Great. I'll put the boys to bed by myself—*again*. That's great, honey. See ya."

If you would have asked me to rate my marriage on a scale of one to ten, I would have said that we were a one . . . or maybe even something closer to a 0.5. I could tell that Dave was totally clueless about this, which, of course, made me even angrier because, honestly, how could he possibly not know how bad we were doing?

Facing My Reality

This was my on and off reality until—before I knew it—ten years had passed. Then out of nowhere, Dave suddenly wanted to make a huge deal out of our tenth anniversary. He took me out to a very nice restaurant—which made me wonder if he had a coupon. After we sat down and the waiter began bringing roses to our table, I could tell that Dave was thinking this was a home run. He began to pour out his heart about the ten years we had spent together, and even I had to admit he was being pretty sweet. He was like a little boy that night as he kept waiting for the next thing he had planned to happen—I could tell he even planned what he was going to say when each rose arrived.

It was a lovely dinner, but it didn't take a rocket scientist to figure out the next part of his plan—ah, the old parking maneuver. *Smooth, Dave . . . real smooth.* I knew Dave Wilson, and I knew there was an ulterior motive to his "parking lot prayer time."

I had made it through the dinner and his planned parade of roses, but the idea of being intimate, passionate, or spontaneous with him in a middle school parking lot was just more than I could handle at that moment. He had "that" look, and I tried to ignore it, but eventually he made his move.

And I was thinking, *Ugh, I can't even . . . I cannot go there.*

He seemed baffled by my lack of affection, which baffled me in return. I wasn't trying to hurt him, but I had no place within me left to hide. You would think that it would have taken the mustering of some sort of courage to say what I said next, but sadly, the words came easily. These were now matters of facts—bricks I had been hauling in my heart for years. I could lug them no longer. Whether he knew it or not, it was now going to be his turn to feel the weight of it all.

"I've lost my feelings for you."

There. I finally said it. I wish the words would have brought me to tears, but they didn't. The look on his face reflected utter shock. He had just planned this romantic evening, but instead he was coming face-to-face with reality—*my* reality. I knew that my words killed him, but I was at a point where I didn't even know what else to say.

He asked me to explain what I meant, so I said, "I feel like you're never home. I feel like you're not engaged with me. I feel like you're not engaged with the boys."

The floodgates were open now. I shared with him how, at first, I was really angry. Then I became really bitter. Then my bitterness turned to resentment. Then after a while, I didn't even care that he was gone. This was the final brick—I honestly no longer cared that he was gone.

I was gone. I had given up. I was in this alone, and now I knew that since I had finally told him, it would be the beginning of the end for our marriage. I waited for his reply, but he said nothing. What could be said? What was done was done.

I don't remember how long we sat there in silence as I waited for his reply, but then Dave said the most bizarre thing: "Honey, I just have to do something first."

Do something? What was he talking about? Was he about to go somewhere?

A Voice from God

When Ann first spoke the words that she had no feelings for me anymore, I (Dave) literally had no idea what she was talking about. Where was this coming from? We had had an incredible evening. I thought our marriage was almost perfect . . . and she thought it was almost over.

When she began to share her heart with me, my initial thoughts were defensive. I knew I could prove to her that she was wrong, and that, in fact, I was home more often than she was giving me credit for. I wanted to prove to her that she and the boys were my top priorities. Believe it or not, I started to reach into the back seat to pull out my weekly planner so I could show her on my written calendar that her perception of me wasn't even close to the truth. By the way, this grabbing for evidence was how I regularly argued with Ann in those days—trying to prove my point rather than listening to hers.

As I reached back, I sensed an internal voice. *Don't you even think about grabbing that thing! Shut up and listen.* Now I didn't hear an audible voice from God, but the nudge of the Holy Spirit in this moment was loud and firm. Actually, it was more of a shove than a nudge.

So I just sat there and listened.

As Ann shared everything she was feeling, I began to realize just how crazy my schedule really was. I began not just to listen, but also to actually hear what she was saying—and what I heard moved my heart past the point of being defensive and into the deep, dark reality that it was true. All of it.

As she continued—and believe me, I did not interrupt even one time—I again sensed that God was speaking to me. It was actually almost mystical at the time. I could hear everything Ann was saying to me, but at the same time, I could also hear God's voice. He said one word.

Repent.

When God told me to repent, I knew exactly what he meant. I wasn't committing some immoral sin or brashly betraying my marriage vows. The call of God to me at that moment was very clear—he was calling me back to my first love. Back to an intimacy *with him* that I had previously known but was no longer living.

I was so busy at that time in my life that I could not remember the last time I had just sat with God and loved him, nor could I remember the last time I had spent time in God's Word just letting him love me. Every time I had gone to the Bible in the last year, it was to prepare a sermon that I could preach to others. Most of my prayers were "help me" prayers as I walked onstage to speak. I had become consumed with my job and no longer consumed with God. In a word, I was lukewarm. I remember growing up in the church and hating lukewarm Christians—and vowing to never become one.

And now I was one of them.

In that moment—the seemingly darkest moment of our marriage—the simple secret we are about to walk out together through the pages of this book began to be revealed to my heart. In that one word—*repent*—I knew God was saying that the only way the "horizontal" human relationship between me as a husband and Ann as a wife could work was if my "vertical" relationship with him was made right. Both are important to God, but the order matters . . . I mean, *really* matters.

The "vertical" *always* comes first.

So as Ann finished sharing her heart, I told her that before I could talk about this any further, I just needed to do something, and I needed to do it, "Right here. Right now."

I knew that before I could respond to what she was saying, I needed to respond to what God was saying. I was finally ready to get these two things properly aligned. I felt that I needed to pray—and on my knees, at that—because I wanted my posture to reflect the seriousness of this surrender.

So that's what I did. I got on my knees in the front seat of that little car, which wasn't easy to do because the steering wheel was pressed against my back. But it had to happen. And then I prayed . . . out loud. "God, I repent. I am lukewarm and am not fully surrendered to you. I want to be the husband, the father, and the man you've called me to be. I will never be that man without you and your power. I resurrender my life and my marriage to you."

On the Floorboard

Dave was going somewhere, all right . . . just not anywhere I (Ann) expected. A moment that should have been the beginning of the end for our marriage was instead the beginning of a new beginning.

I don't even know how he did it. He somehow turned around in our Honda and put his knees on the floorboard—with the steering wheel in his back. I was speechless. Then he began to pray out loud, repenting of being too busy and being lukewarm— begging God to help him become the husband and father he was supposed to be and not the hypocrite he had become.

His knees on the floorboard left me floored as well. I just sat there looking at him, barely able to believe what I was seeing. My heart had become a brick inside of me—but in that moment, it began to break. As he prayed, I could suddenly hear God gently whispering to my soul, *Ann Wilson, you have been trying to get your happiness from your husband, and I never made him for that. I never equipped him to fill all your needs. I am the only One who can meet all your needs.*

I couldn't believe my spiritual ears, but the message was undeniably clear. I hadn't been willing to even kiss my husband of ten years, but when God's words rang out in my heart, I became willing to do something even crazier: I turned around and got on my knees beside Dave. For me, it was a moment of repentance too.

I prayed, "Jesus, I too want to surrender all of my life to you. I've realized tonight that I've been trying to find my life in Dave. I've been trying to get from him what only you—and you alone—can provide. I've believed that if Dave would just be a better husband, *then* I could truly be happy. This is a lie. You are my true source of joy. I choose you again tonight as my life. Take my life and our marriage and do great things in and through us."

Adding the Vertical

It's a crazy story, we know. But this story is the reason you are reading these words—and it revealed to us the secret to a healthy, godly marriage. That night, we began replacing the bricks of bitterness and selfishness we had been lugging around for so long. It was a moment of spiritual awakening for both of us. We asked God to come in and heal us, to give us wisdom to know how to go on from there, and, really, just to change our hearts.

And the craziest part is, he did everything we asked.

As we reminisce some twenty-eight years later, we can tell you that our moment of repentance changed everything . . . and we mean *everything*. The secret we had been missing for the first decade of our marriage began to become our new daily reality—and we now pray that this will begin a new reality for you as well.

Don't dismiss it as too simplistic—the foundational truths of God generally are pretty simple because they are woven into the very fabric of creation. When you finally stumble onto one or more of the deeply divine principles of grace, you will almost always find that they already seem familiar to you—like a pair of gloves that fits perfectly. Before you find them, you figure that maybe your hands are supposed to be cold all the time, and yet you are unsatisfied. But then when a fresh truth from the grace of God shows up in your life, it just fits like a . . . well, you know.

God gives exactly what you never quite knew you always needed.

The simple secret begins with realizing that a purely horizontal marriage just doesn't work. There is no life—no power—in ourselves alone. Adding the Vertical creates area—literally it is *room* for both of you not only to survive marriage, but also to be fulfilled as married people. But without the Vertical—without God in first place—we search for life where there is no life . . . where there is no higher point of grace to create room for growth, forgiveness, and movement.

We realized that as wonderful as we both were as people, we made pretty lousy gods. I (Dave) was trying to find life and happiness through my accomplishments, while I (Ann) was trying to find my joy in Dave being the husband I had always dreamed about. In both cases, no human being can give us what only God possesses.

C. S. Lewis wrote, "If I find in myself a desire which no experience in this world can satisfy, the most probable explanation is that I was made for another world."* Could it be said any better than that? What you and I are looking for cannot be found in the horizontal. It cannot be found in another human being or anywhere else on this planet.

Yes, you know this to be true in theory—so did we before we drove into that parking lot. But the fact that we were "running out of room" proved that our head knowledge was not aligned with our heart experience.

It took a vertical miracle to change our horizontal mess.

You see, after pastoring for years and traveling the country sharing with couples about marriage, we have found that we were not alone. Most people believe that marriage will satisfy us and fulfill us. This promise is constantly reinforced in culture, both Christian and mainstream. Just consider one of the most famous lines in all of pop culture from the movie *Jerry Maguire*.

Yep, we bet you already know the one.

---

* C. S. Lewis, *Mere Christianity* (1943; repr., New York: Macmillan, 1960), 120.

But just to refresh your memory, picture Tom Cruise standing in Renée Zellweger's family room as her book club drones on and on about their latest pick. Jerry Maguire (Cruise) walks in after landing the biggest deal of his professional career and reveals to Dorothy (Zellweger) just how empty it all feels without her. Then comes the epic line: "You complete me." It's a historic moment in the world of chick flicks, the perfect culmination fading quickly into ending credits. Romantic. Poetic. Moving.

Oh, and it's a lie.

Do you know why there was never a *Jerry Maguire 2*? Because Dorothy couldn't have completed Jerry! She may have said, "You had me at *hello*," but she likely would have said *good-bye* after just a few years of being married to that guy, no matter how good-looking or sweet-talking he may have been. He expected of her what no person can give.

You simply can't complete your spouse . . . and they can't complete you. There is no sequel to this approach to marriage. Like ours, yours will quickly fade into the credits—into either a disillusioned marriage or into a divorce you never planned. If you try to find true happiness and joy in horizontal marriage, you will run out of room. Like thousands of others, you will conclude that you married the wrong person—and if you had just married the right person, *then* you would be happy . . . really happy.

It's a lie.

Yes, you can marry the wrong person. However, if you are looking for a person to fill a divine void, then guess what— *every* person is the wrong person. But when the Vertical enters a marriage, it is no longer constrained by the limitations of its two horizontal participants.

Make no mistake—marriage can be nothing less than spectacular. As we are presently approaching our fourth decade of marriage, we honestly cannot imagine it being any better. But after a few bricks to the head, we learned on the floorboard of that car that neither of us was enough to fill the void we were both feeling—and what freedom there was in that realization!

Our happiness is *not* because we are finding life in one another. We both have discovered that true life and joy are found in one place—Jesus. And yes, while we both already knew this in theory, when we truly slipped his grace onto our marriage like a pair of warm gloves, the coldness of the horizontal dissipated forever. Why? Because when he is your source of life, then you can each become givers in your marriage, not just leeches who try to constantly take from each other what neither of you is equipped to give.

If you are at a place in your marriage where, if you were honest with your spouse, you would say something to the effect of, "I've lost my feelings for you," then please stop and pray. God so often uses our disappointments and discouragements to point us to him. Maybe it's time to quit trying to find real life anywhere but from its real source.

Today is your day to get low (maybe even onto a floorboard) so that you can cry out to the One who is higher . . . the One who is vertical. Trust us, when you finally get this vertical relationship with God into the equation, you will be positioned to receive his help in getting the horizontal relationships healthy as well.

Try it—right now. Seriously, go ahead and get on your knees this minute and ask God for help. He loves that kind of prayer, and he is moving to help you this very minute. Don't miss this opportunity. Then let's go on a journey together to discover just what a vertical marriage looks like.*

---

* Check out this link to watch us tell the story that changed our lives and legacy: www.daveandannwilson.com/videostory.

Three

A SURPRISE IN
the Honeymoon Suite

What a day! The day every little girl dreams about was coming to a close . . .

Yes, it was my (Ann's) wedding day.

It was everything I had hoped it would be. By that, I don't really mean that I had the perfect dress, the perfect flowers, or the perfect reception. It was a perfect day because I stood before God and my very best friend to speak vows that would last a lifetime. I felt God's presence as we held each other's hands and looked into each other's eyes. And I truly believed that this good start would ensure smooth sailing for the years to come.

After the wedding, we drove to Columbus, Ohio, where we would spend the first two nights of our two-week adventure. I felt blessed, happy, and humbled—I had just had the privilege of marrying the man of my dreams.

We completed our enchanted hour-and-a-half drive, pulled up to the Hilton entrance, and handed the keys over to the valet. I wish I could have been a bystander watching us as we giddily approached the front desk to check in. I was still wearing my wedding dress, and Dave was still dashing in his tuxedo.

We had only been dating for nine months. This may not seem like a long time, but to us, it was an eternity. You see, we wanted our relationship to be centered on God and were willing to do anything he wanted, which meant that we had decided to remain physically pure in our relationship—and believe me, that was *not* easy!

We were ready for this night, and we couldn't wait to be together. We were giggling—well, I suppose I was the only one giggling as we rode up the elevator. I know my cheeks were flushed because my heart was beating fast.

I just hoped Dave could get me out of this darn dress.

We opened the door to behold the largest hotel room either of us had ever seen in our lives. We walked around the room in amazement—for about five minutes. There were more pressing matters to attend to.

Dave took me in his arms, and we kissed a long, and a long-awaited, unrestrained kiss that was now completely allowed between a husband and wife. Then Dave somehow got me out of my dress . . . but I made him wait just a little bit longer, heading into the bathroom alone to shower after a long day.

I slipped into the bridal lingerie that I had painstakingly picked out and then pulled on the luxurious hotel bathrobe, just to add a little more anticipation. Dave jumped into the shower as well—for a total of two whole minutes. He came out and grabbed my hand, pulling me toward the bed.

But to my surprise, instead of literally tossing me into the bed as I expected, he instead drew me to the end of the bed, took my other hand, and turned me to face him. He looked down at me tenderly and said, "Before we get into bed, I would love for us to kneel before God together and thank him that he brought us together, but more importantly, to offer him our lives together and our marriage. You good with that?"

I was more than good with that! I couldn't think of a better way to start our lives together. So there we were, kneeling together in our white Hilton bathrobes, a young and naive nineteen-year-old and a not much older twenty-two-year-old. Dave continued to hold my hand, fingers intertwined, as we bowed, gently touching our foreheads together.

A sense of quiet awe surrounded us, just as it had back at the church as we spoke our solemn vows to one another, but this was even more personal. No one else was around to hear or witness—no one, that is, but our Father in heaven who loved us.

My young husband began to pray, "Heavenly Father, thank you for an amazing day and for miraculously bringing Ann and me together. I can't believe that you are now allowing us to do life together. I surrender my life to you, and I surrender our marriage to you. We ask that you will use us to impact this world for your purposes. We pray that you will not only give us a *good* marriage, but that you would please give us a *great* marriage!"

I finished the prayer with, "O Lord, I agree with Dave. You have been so faithful and good to us. I surrender my life to you as well, along with our marriage. We will do whatever you want us to do and go wherever you want us to go. Help our marriage to be a light to the world . . . and I agree with Dave, help us to have not just a good marriage, but a great marriage! In Jesus' name we ask these things. Amen."

And then the fireworks began—or at least a few firecrackers.

We didn't know it then, but that wedding night prayer would change the course of our lives. I thought it would guarantee that trouble would go around us and leave us alone. I thought that being so submitted to God in the beginning would pave a pathway of challenge-free romance.

But as you already know, going vertical on our first day of marriage did not exempt us from failure, heartbreak, or disillusionment. But praying that prayer did begin a pattern for us—that whenever we reached a turning point in our relationship, we would always fall to our knees together and rely on Someone other than ourselves to sustain and empower our marriage.

Vertical marriage isn't a one-time deal; it is a daily surrender.

Say What?

Ah, wedded bliss! This was what we were experiencing. Our honeymoon couldn't have gone any better. In fact, time flew by as we dove headfirst into the joys of marriage. Now only three days remained until we would have to leave New Hampshire and head back to Ohio to face "real" life together.

But in my mind, how bad could even "real" life be? I had my perfect and handsome man by my side, so what could go wrong? I had started my part of the marriage with a vertical prayer, but my emotional security was still firmly established in the horizontal plane of a person—and little did I know that he was not and could never be equipped to be my source of security in this life.

That night, I was fast asleep when all of a sudden, I was awakened by someone calling my name. It startled me so much that I sat straight up in bed. I looked at Dave, thinking he had called my name, but he was still sound asleep. As I looked around the room, I felt a sense of hushed holiness. It is difficult to describe, but I somehow knew that God wanted to speak to me, so I climbed out of bed feeling awe and wonder. The old wooden floors of the cottage creaked beneath my feet as I knelt on the faded braided rug.

With hands folded and head bowed all the way down to my knees, I whispered out loud, "I'm here, Lord."

Without a single second's delay, I heard a strong, clear voice in my head. "Ann, read the book of James."

That was it. Nothing else. The hushed holiness dissipated as I waited to see if there was anything else. *Nope. Nada. Humph. Well, that was weird,* I thought as I climbed back into bed and cuddled up next to Dave. *What was that all about?* I mused as I began to drift back to sleep. As a new Christian, I didn't know what the book of James was about, but I hoped it included something about God making all your dreams come true. Yes, that was my last thought before falling back asleep.

The next morning, I slept in late, made a hearty breakfast for my new husband, and went outside, where we both read our Bibles and spent a little time praying. As we sat on our chairs facing the gorgeous Winnisquam Lake, I recounted to Dave what had happened to me in the middle of the night.

"That's kind of weird," he said, as puzzled as I was.

"What's the book of James about?" I asked Dave. We were both young in our relationships with God. Neither of us had grown up in homes where spiritual matters were discussed very much.

"I'm not positive, but I think it's about going through hard times."

I opened my Bible and flipped to the back, recalling that it was toward the end somewhere.

"Found it!" I said happily. "Why don't I read it out loud and then we can talk about it?" I suggested.

Dave nodded, so off I went, reading the first five verses of James 1:

> James, a servant of God and of the Lord Jesus Christ.
> To the twelve tribes scattered among the nations:
> Greetings.

Consider it pure joy, my brothers and sisters, whenever you face trials of many kinds, because you know that the testing of your faith produces perseverance. Let perseverance finish its work so that you may be mature and complete, not lacking anything. If any of you lacks wisdom, you should ask God, who gives generously to all without finding fault, and it will be given to you.

My mind was reeling. *Wait, what? Where's the part that says if you follow Jesus, he will make you healthy, happy, and wise? Is this some sort of practical joke, God? I'm on my honeymoon, for goodness' sake! We're supposed to be making love and dreaming about our future together!*

Dave and I sat in silence for a few minutes.

"Why do you think God would wake me up to tell me to read such a depressing book?" I asked Dave.

He replied, "I have no idea."

All of it was just a little too weighty to ponder on that spectacularly sunny day. So I tucked it away in the far recesses of my mind, hoping I wouldn't need to retrieve it anytime soon.

Sacrificing My Life

Three months passed, and things were going pretty well. The honeymoon was behind us, and we were living with *our* parents (you heard me right—not just *my* parents or *his* parents) in Ohio. We were working hard to raise our support so that we could report to the University of Nebraska and join the Campus Crusade for Christ staff as their new Athletes in Action field representatives. Raising our financial support was by no means easy, but we were amazed at how much money God was already supplying—and we were grateful for the incredible people we were meeting along the way. But yes, we were living with *our* parents. We went back and forth between our parents' houses, depending on that week's needs.

This particular week, we were staying with Dave's single mom—Janiece's Honeymoon Suite, as she dubbed it. One night after Dave and I had already been in bed for several hours, the exact same scenario played out again, just as it had on our honeymoon.

"Ann!" It was the voice again, waking me up.

The same hushed holiness was near again—the sense of God being present and desiring to speak to me. I knew what to do this time, so I quietly threw back the covers and knelt beside the bed.

"I'm here, Jesus. What do you want to say to me?" I asked humbly with my head bowed low.

As clear as if someone was whispering directly into my ear, I heard, "Ann, would you be willing to die for me?"

I could sense that this was no joke. I felt the heaviness of the moment deep in my gut. Fear began to rise from my chest and make its way into my head. I repeated in my head what I thought I had heard. "Would I die for Jesus?"

"Lord," I frantically whispered, "are you asking me if I would die for you literally?"

"Ann," I heard once again, "would you be willing to die for me?"

I wish I could tell you that my response was selfless and holy, but that would be a lie. "Uh, well . . . no, Jesus, not right now! I'm only nineteen, and I just got married. I have a whole life to live! How can I have kids or have an impact on this world if I die now?"

Then his question became a little more specific. "Will you die for me and sacrifice your life so that I can make Dave the man I want him to be?"

Now *this* was going too far! I wanted to serve Jesus—to love him and tell everyone I knew about him, but to actually die of some horrible disease or in a fatal car crash just so Dave Wilson could become some godly dude and be used by God in amazing ways? No thank you.

Then my mind went there. I imagined Dave at my funeral—crying, broken, and devastated, all the while giving Jesus all he had and eventually becoming this great man—*without* me by his side. Was I willing to let that happen? The answer was still no. I began to cry, begging God not to take me. I begged him to use us together, not apart.

"Ann, will you die for me and sacrifice your life so that I can make Dave the man I want him to be?"

I continued to softly cry as God persistently asked the same question again. I loved Jesus so much. He had given his life so that I might live. He had given me a joy and purpose that was unimaginable. I was young in my faith, but I knew I could trust God with my life, my marriage, my future, and my death. He was a good God and only wanted me to benefit from my relationship with him. As I listened to the question, instead of flatly rejecting it, I began to ponder it. Did I love him enough and trust him enough to offer my life as a living sacrifice in order for Dave to become the man he wanted? If this was a part of God's purpose for my life, was I willing to live—or die—for that purpose?

It took some time, but slowly a sense of resolve began growing within me, rising like a wave moving toward the shore. It brought me courage, helping me to make up my mind. I was still scared. I was still hurt.

But I wiped away my tears and earnestly whispered, "Jesus, I give my life to you . . . and yes, I give up my life so you can make Dave the man you want him to be."

I had said it. Then I began to cry again at the thought of

leaving all I knew and loved on this earth, fully expecting God to take me at any moment. I waited as the seconds and minutes ticked by, but there was nothing but silence.

Suddenly, I heard the now familiar voice. "Ann, I'm not going to take your life, but there will be times during this next year that you will wish I had. The coming year will be filled with trials and difficulties, but I want you to know that I am with you and will use these circumstances to begin making Dave the man I want him to be. These trials will shape you both to look more like me—and they will teach you to depend on me."

As soon as I knew I wasn't going to actually die that night or anytime soon, relief flooded my heart. I knew what he had said about trials, but anything would be better than dying, right? In fact, I really didn't spend a lot of time pondering those prophetic words. They didn't wash over my soul until a few months later, when those trials actually began.

Refined by Fire

Looking back on that unforgettable night, I now can't help but be grateful for God's gracious warning of the battle that was about to begin in our lives and marriage. His words came true, and life became unbearably hard. That night forever marked me, but I will admit to you that it didn't make the trials we were about to face any easier. It just made me aware that God was not far away; he was in it with us.

Yes, as we begin to really drill down into the concepts of marriage, it would be all too easy to rattle off clever stories and tips about how to communicate or how to spice up the bedroom. But the truth is, marriage is not at all easy. It is a matter of life and death—which is why your vows reflect this truth in the words, "Until death do us part."

Before you read any further, you don't need to be awakened by what sounds like an audible voice deep down in your soul. Trust me, it is evident from the Scriptures that God is asking you the same question he asked me. Are you willing to lose everything you have and think you want so that God can give you—and your spouse—everything he wants and knows you need? Can you trust that his dreams for your marriage are higher than your own, even if they lead you through difficult moments?

The evangelist Luke says it so clearly: "For whoever wants to save their life will lose it, but whoever loses their life for me will save it" (9:24). You don't have to physically die to lose your life; you just have to listen, trust, and be willing to let Someone else take the reins of your dreams, direction, and, ultimately, your marriage itself. And yes, since you are now "one" with your spouse, what God does in your life will also be a very effective tool for doing something significant in your spouse's life. Iron will sharpen iron—and sometimes sparks will fly.

You don't have to feel ready or able; you just have to be willing. That's all. God doesn't need you to be brave, only willing. He doesn't need you to be qualified; he'll qualify you through his process and plan. Just listen and be willing, knowing that losing yourself is something you can say yes to, because you trust that the life he has for you is infinitely greater than the life you have planned for yourself.

Vertical marriage is a place where you lose yourself—not necessarily in the dreams and ambitions of your spouse, but rather in the dreams and direction of a trustworthy Father. He's not trying to destroy you; he's trying to refine you. The most precious metals are shaped in the fire, and it seems that we, God's precious children, are shaped in the same way.

Are you willing to die? If so, get ready to live.

Four

THE VERTICAL
Starts Here

God's words to Ann came true; our first year of marriage was filled with lots of pain. We were up most evenings past midnight trying to resolve conflicts. I (Dave) was convinced that Ann was selfish and wrong—and of course *I* wasn't either of those things. I would constantly yell to convince her that, once again, I was right. I just couldn't understand why she was so "needy" and felt so unloved by me. I was exhausted trying to meet all her many needs, and she was frustrated that I was so "clueless." We constantly hurt each other with our harsh words and selfish actions.

Just nine months in, Ann and I were in another of our daily conflicts that never seemed to get resolved. After finally giving up and going to bed, I found myself wide awake at 2 a.m., so I went downstairs and opened the Bible to seek God's help.

As I read the apostle Paul's famous statement, "to live is Christ and to die is gain" (Philippians 1:21), I was struck with this thought: *I would rather be dead than married to Ann.* Believe it or not, that's how hard our marriage had become in just nine short months. If you would have told me on our wedding day that I would have ever felt this way, let alone in less than a year, I would have told you you were crazy. But I've also talked with hundreds of husbands and wives who can relate. The first year of marriage is notoriously difficult, but the trials came as a complete shock to us.

When Ann came downstairs to see what I was doing, she seemed pleased to see that I was in God's Word, but then I told her what I had just prayed. I literally said, "I just told God that I'd rather die than be married to you." (By the way, *not* a good thing to ever say to your spouse!) As you can imagine, my words crushed her. I was just trying to be completely honest, because the truth of those words in that moment was painfully real. What God had previously revealed to Ann was now a reality.

And yet he was *right there*, ready to begin a miracle.

From Death to Life

Over the years of our marriage, Ann and I often faced what at the time felt like death. The death of our dreams. The death of our expectations. The death of our love. In fact, the only reason we are still together is that there was—and is—a very loving and personal Father who intervened to transform each of our lives and personalities. And through this unlikely love triangle, an amazing life together emerged from those moments of seeming death.

This is the wonderful mystery of what God promises to do in the lives—and the marriages—of his people. He takes weeping that has lasted all night and somehow turns it into a joyful morning of rejoicing. He takes ashes—the final, worthless thing that remains when everything has burned to the ground—and produces something beautiful. Yes, he transforms death into life. This is not just a metaphor; this is literally what God does. That's the only reason we are still here and still married—happily, by the way. In fact, as I'm writing this, I just asked Ann again, and she said we are now a 9.9 on the marriage scale.

Of course, she is wrong again—we are a ten!

You don't have to be perfect for God to do this kind of daily miracle in your life or marriage. We certainly are not. You can be severely flawed. Angry. Addicted. Apathetic. Even atheistic. From each of these positions, you are still being targeted by grace. You are still in the sights of the Savior. There is no need to clean up your marriage before you can fully trust in the Vertical to begin being active in your story.

The very fact that you are reading these words is evidence that you are being pursued by grace—what great news! Even when I had been a negligent husband and father, driving away the feelings my wife once had for me, Christ was pursuing me. He never stopped caring, even when my hypocrisy was at cataclysmic levels. I never deserved his vertical attention—and I still don't. And yet he never stops.

The right place to begin is *not* the simple application of relational tips, tricks, or takeaways. Neither is it addressing every single problem in your marriage so that each faux pas can be meticulously attacked with all the energy each of you can muster—trust me, this approach will leave you exhausted, because treating your marriage like a work project can demolish the very relational parts you are trying to salvage.

No, the right place to begin is to start with *Jesus*. Believe rightly and fully that God's grace in Christ is being extended to you, regardless of how distant, unworthy, or dirty you feel.

We could easily coach you to work harder to make a better marriage, but this approach alone will never produce a vertical story or a vertical marriage. Self-discipline is great, but it doesn't transform hearts; only Christ can do that. First you need to abandon yourself to God's love for you. Trust in God first, and you will be inviting all that only *God* can do in your life and marriage.

Once you've trusted in God, you'll be ready to tackle your marriage—but all your efforts will actually work, because God's Holy Spirit will be empowering your thoughts and deeds.

Out of Alignment

Go back to the floorboard story with me—you know, the night I literally almost lost my marriage. Consider how crazy it was that, at that point, I was already ten years into pastoring and telling others about Christ and his message. Come on, I was literally a professional Christian! I would have told you—and fully believed—that I was "all in" with God. How could I not have been?

But the truth is, those would have been just words.

I was preaching a fairly good game, but I wasn't living it. I'm not saying I was not a Christian, but my daily walk with God had become pretty much nonexistent. I was running from event to event, meeting to meeting, and ministry opportunity to ministry opportunity *for* God, but I was no longer allowing or fostering the cultivation of a relationship *with* God. God had become my career path rather than the beating passion of my heart. His love was still present and I loved him in return, but pleasing him was no longer my highest purpose.

I would have told you that my priorities were perfectly aligned in the classic, proper order: God, family, and *then* my job. It made for a great sermon, but that's all it had become to me. In reality, my life was aligned in exactly the opposite order: job, family, and *then* God.

To be clear, having a job or being busy is not a sin. We all have to juggle responsibilities. I'm not saying that each of us should spend all day every day sitting with our Bible and listening to worship music. This is not a call to stop living your life—but I was missing the life in all my living.

My schedule was merely a symptom of the more imminent problem. My daily calendar revolved around work, even when my work did not require such uncontested devotion. In other words, I not only refused to say no, but I also became addicted to seeking out more things that would help me stay busy. I became accustomed—perhaps even addicted—to the pace of it all, allowing it to replace my higher priorities. It became easier to just stay busy going about the work of God than to really address my actual relationship with God.

I was doing God's work, but I did not really know well the One for whom I was working. Ever been there?

So now you can see how my floorboard confession was a watershed moment. I was finally coming to grips with the life I had been living under the guise of ministry. But there was still a great danger that I would speak the right things but never actually allow these things to change me. How was I going to follow through? How was I going to not just proclaim that I was all in with my relationship with Christ, but actually continue to believe and pursue this proclamation?

Even I knew that if my floorboard confession wasn't followed up by concrete actions, there would be severe consequences to follow, not the least of which would be the loss of my marriage.

I know it sounds a little weird, but that night, something inside of me on a "belief" level was transformed. I didn't just get up and try harder; I actually fell back in love with Jesus. Realizing how far I had wandered from him, I felt an intense desire to be close to him, to recommit myself to him, and to sacrifice my own selfish desires so I could please him. My relationship with

God suddenly lost some of its immaturity—its myopic focus on the daily, career-driven details and responsibilities.

In a way, I guess you could say I started dating God again. When you go out on a date with someone, you spend time together so that you can both get to know each other better. The truth is, I had not just sat with Jesus in months because I had not made the time. Again, this was not a salvation issue; it was a closeness issue. Just like my marriage, I was still in a relationship with Jesus, but I wasn't being very present. I was a million miles away, wrapped up in my own little reality where everything revolved around me—and trust me, no human can sustain being the center of the solar system.

For the first time in a long time, I wanted to orbit God's reality. He became the actual center of my life's pursuits.

A Workout Program

In many ways, the events of that night held up a mirror, allowing me to see my true condition. Can you relate? Have you ever avoided really looking at yourself in the mirror because you wanted to just keep eating whatever your heart desired and sit around bingeing Netflix or surfing the internet?

I've been there.

Years ago, I looked in the mirror and had one of those "What is that?" moments. I had gone from college athlete to soft and flabby. Oh man, it hurt to see myself that way, but when I did, I decided right then and there that I had to do something radical. So I bought the DVD for P90X, a grueling workout program that features an insane number of push-ups and pull-ups. The first day, I could do only one pull-up. *One!* Meanwhile, my college-age, football-playing son cranked out thirty-five straight pull-ups without breaking a sweat. He even did a few one-armed pull-ups! Talk about embarrassing for Mr. One Push-up Man—scratch that, Push-up Boy.

Needless to say, I felt like a total loser. *I can only do one pull-up? Are you kidding me?* I decided to use my son's display of awesomeness as motivation. I committed to P90X every day for the next ninety days to see what kind of results I could achieve.

By the end of the month, I was doing twenty pull-ups! I honestly couldn't believe my progress. And Ann couldn't believe it either as she started chasing me around the house to get a closer look at my new body! Okay, maybe I made up that last part.

But how did I get this new body? It's really simple. First, I believed differently, and then I let that belief lead me into the right kind of work—every day.

It's really no different in our walk with God. Just *trying harder* to be like Jesus doesn't work. I can't tell you the number of times I've sat in church and been inspired by some new truth, deciding right then and there to become a new man—a better husband, father, and leader. I would then run out and try harder to reach that goal, but it never worked. You can't "try harder" yourself into walking with God. Many in the church spend their whole lives trying harder under their own power to become more like Jesus. It just doesn't work!

But *training smarter* does—beginning with a right understanding of God's grace and work in our lives. He is working in us, so we can be free to "work out" in our spiritual training. As the apostle Paul writes to the Philippians, "Therefore, my dear friends, as you have always obeyed—not only in my presence, but now much more in my absence—continue to *work out your salvation* with fear and trembling, for it is *God who works in you* to will and to act in order to fulfill his good purpose" (Philippians 2:12–13, emphasis mine). You see, Paul reminds us to work, but to keep in mind that as we do so, God is also working something higher in us at the same time. This is great news! If you can't do the pull-up, he can do it for you!

We know that physical training involves exercises that develop our strength, flexibility, and aerobic conditioning. But how do we "work out" spiritually? It's simple. Spiritual training involves the classic disciplines of the Christian life: prayer, Bible study, meditation, fasting, worship, acts of service, tithing, and so on. Each of these practices exercises the muscles of our faith, making us stronger, pushing us to be more flexible, and giving us greater endurance.

Yes, there is work for us to do here, but don't fall into the trap of thinking that everything is up to you. That is not a vertical perspective.

These spiritual disciplines help us take the appropriate posture before God so he can transform us. And just like my P90X experience, transformation takes time . . . and work. Here are some additional thoughts on spiritual training.

Day 1 Is Usually Embarrassing

Any time you start a new workout after a long period of rest, it is usually very hard and very embarrassing. At first, you can't really do much in the gym—maybe not even a single pull-up—because you are out of shape.

So what!

You can't start anywhere else but where you are. So start where you *are*, not where you think you are or where you wish you were. Just get moving and eventually you will make progress. But you have to be willing to start or else you'll never be able to stay at it.

When I attended my first Bible study in college, I didn't know the difference between the Old Testament and the New

Testament. I actually thought one part was for old people and the other was for us youngsters. When the leader asked us to turn to a book in the Bible, I had no idea where to look—so I went to the table of contents and looked for a page number. Everybody else was way ahead of me, and it felt super embarrassing.

But guess what? I didn't quit. I kept training, and now I'm the world's greatest Bible scholar! (Just making sure you're still paying attention.)

Day 2 Is All about "Want To"

The main question to answer on the second day of training is, "How bad do you want it?" You will wake up sore from the first day's efforts. The excitement will be gone, and it will be hard to get back to it.

So what do you do?

You get out of bed and go back to the gym. It is no different with your spiritual walk. Get your Bible open and start reading, even if you aren't really "feeling it." Feelings are not required for God to show up and reveal himself to you in a fresh new way. As you see who he is again and again, you will fall back in love with him in a way that transcends simple emotions, feelings, impressions, or expectations. Deciding to keep going will help you break the cycle of emotional expectation that is unhealthy and instead lead you to the healthy expectation that God is always present, approachable, and active in your life, regardless of how you feel.

The path to godliness includes a will to *train daily*, especially when we don't feel like it. Greatness doesn't just come to us; it is grabbed daily by those who truly want it with everything they have. If we train ourselves daily to become a man or woman of God, he will meet us right where we are and take us to the goal we could never reach on our own.

Paul writes to the Corinthian church about the strong commitment and desire of the athletes of their time. These athletes would pay whatever price it took to win a medal in their Olympic-style games. He then compares this commitment to win something that has no eternal value to our commitment to Jesus, which has immense eternal value:

> Do you not know that in a race all the runners run, but only one gets the prize? Run in such a way as to get the prize. Everyone who competes in the games goes into strict training. They do it to get a crown that will not last, but we do it to get a crown that will last forever. Therefore I do not run like someone running aimlessly; I do not fight like a boxer beating the air. No, I strike a blow to my body and make it my slave so that after I have preached to others, I myself will not be disqualified for the prize.
>
> 1 Corinthians 9:24–27

The question is not about how strong you presently are, but rather how badly you want to know Jesus better and see him continually transform your life. If you want a great marriage, then it starts right here, right now, with *you*. Get your eyes off of your spouse and what they are doing or not doing. Put your eyes on yourself. You can begin to change your marriage—starting right now—by getting yourself back into the daily disciplines of becoming who God created you to be.

Don't just wander aimlessly; run to win—today!

DAY 3 IS ALL ABOUT "HOW TO"

Decades ago, I heard the now well-known author and pastor Rick Warren talk about how we can best grow spiritually. He described this in a way I've never forgotten and in a way that applies just as well to our marriages as it does to our vertical walk with God.

If you and I want to walk with Jesus and fall more in love with our spouses, we need to train daily, weekly, and annually. I adapted this concept to remember it this way:

- Divert Daily (DD)
- Withdraw Weekly (WW)
- Abandon Annually (AA)

Here are some suggestions on how to do this.

Divert Daily

To grow in my relationship with Jesus, I need to train daily. At least once every day, I need to "divert" from my regular routine and carve out some alone time with Jesus. For almost forty years now, I have made a habit out of spending some time in God's Word each day. I follow a daily Bible reading and study program that helps deepen my walk with God. I also endeavor to pray daily as well.

Though no one will be perfect in these disciplines in terms of consistency, this daily diversion is time that I try to build into my schedule as a priority. If I want to be the man, husband, and father that God is calling me to be, then I must "divert daily" to allow God time and space to cultivate these things in me.

It will not "just happen." You don't get six-pack abs without working out daily, and the same is true of our relationship with God. I can talk all I want about getting in shape, but there will be no serious results until I get into the gym every day.

The same is true in our vertical walks—and the same is true for our marriages. The best marriages "divert daily" as well. All of our lives are crazy busy, but if we want our marriage to grow, then we must "train" daily. Ann and I developed a training habit early in our marriage of trying to spend at least fifteen minutes talking each day. For us, this means not turning on the TV until we've spent some time communicating about our relationship.

Have we done it every single day? No. But we do make it a high priority and have made it happen most of the time. Of course, when our kids were little, it was tough since we often felt like we were barely surviving, but somehow, we still managed to carve out this time on most days.

And trust me, it was worth it.

Withdraw Weekly

Now we move on to a weekly rhythm. If we want to grow spiritually, God has commanded that we pause at least once a week to unplug from everything and simply rest in our vertical relationship with him, trusting that he has everything in this world under control. This practice is called Sabbath, and believe it or not, it is so important to God that it even made his all-time top ten list!

God put rest and relaxation up there as some of the most important things we can do if we want to live healthy, stable lives. Pulling away from our hectic pace for one day a week is critically important for our spiritual health, and for our physical health as well. As a pastor, this one is easy to preach and difficult to live. Yet when I violate the Sabbath principle, my vertical relationship with God suffers—and so do my physical and emotional health.

I have learned to build this day of rest into my schedule. Without it, I eventually implode and become a bear to live with—it's almost as if God knew what he was talking about. The bottom line is, we are created to take a day off every week.

Try it. Take a day off this week and see how much better you feel. That, my friend, is a gift from your Creator.

But this "withdraw weekly" principle applies to our marriages too. Ann and I were told by our first marriage mentors that the best marriages date weekly. We were so young and clueless that we just believed them, deciding to build a weekly date night into our calendar. The result is that we have been dating each other weekly for almost forty years now.

Have we missed some weeks here and there? Yes, but not many. We know how crucial this time is to our marriage. When the boys were young, I made it my job (not Ann's) to secure the babysitter and plan the date. Ann was fried most of the time from being a young mom, so I felt that it was up to me to get her out of the house for our date. She deserved it. Often she resisted leaving the kids, but once we got out of the house, she was always thankful that we had taken the time together.

I've learned a thing or two about dates as well. My perfect date would be pretty simple—grab a quick bite at a somewhat inexpensive (i.e., cheap) restaurant, hit an action flick, and then go make love somewhere . . . anywhere works for me!

Not so much for Ann. She wants to sit and taaalk at a nice (i.e., expensive) restaurant. Then taaalk some more about our relationship. Then maybe see a nice chick flick and then taaalk some more about how wonderful that guy in the movie was to his girl. Then head home and taaalk some more while I give her a back rub—for an hour!

I'm kidding about Ann's date . . . a little. But the truth is that when we "train" weekly in our relationship, it deeply affects the state of our marriage. If you haven't made "withdraw weekly" a part of your spiritual life and your marriage, then start this week.

I really mean it. Pull out your calendar and write it in—now.

Abandon Annually

The final piece of training for a deeper vertical relationship with God is to get away at least once a year for a spiritual retreat. Go to a men's retreat or a women's retreat, or simply any kind of vertical time away. It will do wonders to refresh your perspective in your relationship with God. Every time I get away from the craziness of my life and schedule to simply focus solely on my walk with God, good things happen. I come back home a better man, husband, father, and leader.

The same is true for your marriage. At least once a year, go away on a vacation for just the two of you. Do not take the kids, and do not take another couple. Just the two of you. Relax. Play. Laugh. Dance. Make love somewhere besides your own bed—it does wonders for your marriage.

Another great idea for a relational boost is to go to a marriage retreat. You will grow both vertically with God and horizontally with each other. Ann and I speak at these all over the country, and we are always amazed at the number of couples who say that this is their first time away in decades. For your marriage to thrive, you must give it time . . . away.

I remember sitting in a lounge chair on a beach in Mexico with Ann right beside me. I also remember that I didn't want to spend the money on this trip (I know, shocker, right). As we were sitting there relaxing and enjoying God's amazing sunset, she reached over and grabbed my hand. She then just simply said, "Marrying you was the greatest decision of my life."

That moment is still perched in the front of my brain. I will never forget it. And trust me, those words are probably not as easily spoken by Ann unless we are sitting together on a beach fully relaxed and able to enjoy one another in an unrushed setting.

It might be time to call the travel agent right now.

PART TWO

Conflict and Communication

Five

"COME BACK HERE AND
Fight Like a Man!"

Like most young couples on their wedding day, we were starry-eyed lovers who had not a care in the world. Elated to begin our life together, we had no doubt that the days ahead would consist of happy, beautiful, matrimonial bliss. After all, we both loved Jesus, and we were confident that God had brought us together as husband and wife.

What could go wrong?

It may not be easy to admit, but the unfortunate truth is that our wedding day was the first day of the worst year of our lives. We were like two trucks on a highway both driving blind with no headlights—and we were about to experience a traumatic head-on collision at the ever-dangerous speed of life. No seat belts. No air bags.

No clue what was about to hit us.

Although it's difficult to boil our issues down to just one problem, it seems pretty evident that the most urgent issue was that we hardly knew each other. Well, perhaps the one even more urgent than that was that we hardly knew *ourselves*. How are you supposed to get to know someone else in such an intimate and intrusive environment when you have yet to fully discover your own worth and identity? Our idyllic pleasure cruise brought with it a cargo of powder kegs stowed away deep under the main deck, just waiting to go *boom*.

Needless to say, we found ourselves in constant conflict, which generally led to lots of shouting and screaming at each other. Up to that point, no one had ever prepared us for the conflict that inevitably occurs in any close relationship, much less in the closest of all relationships. We thought it odd to be at odds, which stacked the odds against us.

But it doesn't have to be that way for you. Having the appropriate expectations and tools for resolving conflict in marriage can defuse the bombs below deck in your marriage. This is why these chapters on communication and resolving conflict are critical to the health and future of your marriage. John Gottman, a leading marriage authority, has discovered that one of the leading predictors of whether a marriage goes the distance is how the married couple handles conflict.*

If we had kept doing our marriage the way we did in the first year, we would have never made it to year thirty-eight. We invite you to read closely and apply diligently as we share some life-changing truths that changed us and will hopefully transform your marriage as well.

Four Patterns of Conflict Resolution

One of the first things we learned (the hard way) about conflict resolution is that all of us approach it with different patterns

---

* See Sybil Carrère and John Mordechai Gottman, "Predicting Divorce among Newlyweds from the First Three Minutes of a Marital Conflict Discussion," *Family Process* 38, no. 3 (September 1999): 293–301, http://joe.ramfeezled.com/wp-content/docs/Carrere-Gottman1999-Predict-divorce-in-3-mins.pdf.

or styles. We often copy what we witnessed in our homes as children. We may also function out of beliefs that we subconsciously hold regarding conflict. There are four basic patterns of conflict resolution in which we all fall.

WIN. A winner is usually good at conflict. Winners actually like conflict and are skilled at winning the argument. They bring eyewitness accounts and evidence, complete with full-color pictures, proving they are right. This is an exaggeration, but only slightly.

YIELD. A yielder will "give in" to bring harmony to the relationship. Yielders believe that the marriage is more important than this one, isolated conflict, so they yield to bring peace back to the marriage.

WITHDRAW. A withdrawer hates conflict. Withdrawers will do whatever it takes to stay away from conflict. If they can leave the room, consider them gone. But if leaving is not possible, they will shut down emotionally instead. It is very difficult to get them to even engage in the conflict.

RESOLVE. A resolver will do whatever it takes to arrive at resolution. Resolvers can't stand to live life without their conflicts being resolved. It takes a lot of work, but they will roll up their sleeves and get it done in whatever way possible.

Can you guess what patterns we brought into our marriage? Ann was a winner. She grew up in a home where conflict was dealt with quickly and regularly. Her parents and siblings just "put it out there" and handled conflicts as they arose. She likes a good fight.

Dave, on the other hand, grew up in a home where conflicts got loud and ugly. Usually there was alcohol involved, and those fights eventually ended in an ugly divorce. This led him to believe that all conflicts are bad and should be avoided at all costs.

So we walked into our marriage having no idea that a *winner* and a *withdrawer* were now required to handle conflict together in a healthy, God-honoring way. Good luck with that!

Under Pressure

As young newlyweds, we moved into Ann's parents' house in Findlay, Ohio, for the first few months of our marriage. Living with your in-laws? Now *that's* pressure. At the time, we were also raising our financial support to join the ministry of Athletes in Action. That was even more pressure.

The pressure just seemed to be too much. We distinctly recall one memorable hot summer day when Ann's parents had gone out for some reason. What should have been prime "newlywed alone time" descended instead into something else altogether. The conflict began, as most conflicts do, with a conversation that eventually escalated into an argument.

When things reached their boiling point, Dave pulled a classic withdrawer move—he got up and walked out of the room. But Ann wasn't done with him, so she followed behind him and shouted, "Hey, where are you going? Come back here and fight like a man!"

Like a man?

Oh no, she didn't.

As manliness went, Dave considered himself to be the manliest of them all. After all, he was the quarterback on his high school and college football teams and was even voted "the man" in his high school and college Halls of Fame. And yet Ann had the audacity to challenge his masculinity! The problem was, as manly as he may have been at the time, he had never resolved a single, solitary conflict in his entire life. His physical muscles were respectable, but his emotional ones were pitiful.

So he did what any born-again, Bible-believing Christian missionary would do. He turned, kept walking away from her, and simply yelled, "Bleep you!"

Except there was no bleep—it was no surprise that Dave copied identically how he had seen his dad handle conflict.

From behind him, he heard Ann scream back, "Oh, yeah? Well, bleep bleep you!"

Whoa. He spun around, totally shocked that his innocent, angelic bride had just double-cursed him. We can only imagine what the neighbors were thinking, since the windows were wide open: "Oh, that's just that missionary couple over there having a nice conversation."

As soon as Ann's words hit the air, Dave stomped upstairs to get away from this horrible thing called marital conflict, but Ann seemed intent on dragging it out. She followed him up the stairs.

"Dave, we've got to talk," she said. "We've got to work this out."

Since Ann's family regularly addressed conflict head-on, she was pursuing this one like she had always done. In her family, you put on your boxing gloves and punched it out until the smoke cleared and all was well again. She just couldn't understand why Dave was taking a dive instead of fighting. To her, it was almost as if his *unwillingness* to keep saying horrible things in this fight was worse than *actually saying* horrible things in this fight.

Trapped, Dave stammered, "What are you doing? Leave me alone!" He felt completely uncomfortable, since resolving conflict was not something he had ever seen done before. The Wilsons didn't face their issues; they buried them and lived to face them another day . . . which never came.

Dave had become really good at running from conflict.

If arguments ever began to surface with a girlfriend, he simply dropped her like a bad habit. Why deal with the trouble, no matter what the rewards might be?

But this version of life—the adult version—wasn't shaping up to be so simple with Ann.

And so unresolved conflict became commonplace in our young marriage, much to Ann's chagrin. We eventually finished raising our financial support and moved to Lincoln, Nebraska, but even so, our inaugural year from hell continued behind closed doors. Dave became the chaplain of the Nebraska Cornhuskers football team, but that didn't help our problems either. In fact, on our drive to Lincoln, another argument ensued. Let's just say that it didn't go well at all, so much so that Ann finally said, "Marrying you was the biggest mistake of my life!" We literally had to pull over and get out of the car so we could both cool down.

The months flew by, and we continued fighting. Dave still wasn't very good at resolving conflict, but in ministry he had at least learned that the Bible says we shouldn't go to bed angry. So we would argue late into the night, which we're sure is exactly what God had in mind when he inspired that particular verse to be written. Not! On the outside, everything looked perfect; but on the inside, we were sinking fast, with no hope in sight.

This is when the 2 a.m. "I would rather be dead than married to you" story we shared earlier happened.

Removing the Blinders

This conversation was one of the lowest moments of our marriage. We just couldn't figure out what had happened. In only a few short months, we had gone from gazing lovingly into each other's eyes to glaring at each other with anger and disgust, each wondering—and often not only to ourselves—if we had married the wrong person.

It may not happen to every couple so quickly, but at some point in marriage, the blinders are removed from your eyes and you begin to realize that this person you have married is not just slightly flawed, but is actually full of flaws. This would be hard enough to swallow, but usually there is something else that happens that doubles the trouble you are experiencing: your spouse has the same realization about you at the same time you are having it about them. Double whammy. It may not always happen to the degree that arguments escalate as ours did, but it always happens—and yet most couples are blindsided when the blinders come off. No one has prepared them for the difficulty, the work, and the unexpected beauty that can arise from marital conflict.

This is why we have literally had hundreds of couples tell us that they believe they married the wrong person—at some point, it happens to almost all of us.

In his book *The Meaning of Marriage*, Timothy Keller says it well: "I'm tired of listening to sentimental talks on marriage. At weddings, in church, and in Sunday school, much of what I've heard on the subject has as much depth as a Hallmark card. While marriage is many things, it is anything *but* sentimental. Marriage is glorious but hard. It's a burning joy and strength, and yet it is also blood, sweat, and tears, humbling defeats and exhausting victories. No marriage I know more than a few weeks old could be described as a fairy tale come true."*

The fact is that every married couple will have conflict—and perhaps a lot of it. That has certainly been true for us. We are

---

* Timothy Keller with Kathy Keller, *The Meaning of Marriage: Facing the Complexities of Commitment with the Wisdom of God* (New York: Riverhead, 2013), 13.

both stubborn, willful, selfish people. There are situations in which one spouse possesses strong personality traits, while the other tends to be more docile or passive. In these situations, it may take longer for the "fuse" to ignite the powder keg, because a pattern has been established of one spouse dominating the other in moments of conflict, but the person being dominated is complicit in the whole affair because such is their default setting when it comes to matters of conflict. But make no mistake, even in situations such as these, a lack of healthy boundaries agreed on by both spouses will eventually cause the fuse to reach the gunpowder, even if it takes years. And then . . .

Boom!

In our marriage, we've learned the hard way that *how we handle conflict will determine the health and future of our marriage.*

It is only by the intervention of a gracious God that we didn't give up on our marriage during that terrible first year. We entered marriage woefully unprepared, but we slowly learned how to handle our emotions, how to confront one another in more loving and constructive ways, how to forgive, and, most importantly, how to trust God—even in those ugly moments when there weren't enough "bleeps" to go around. If we had not allowed God to speak to us through the Scriptures and through his people, we don't know where we would be today.

Conflict Is Normal . . . and Ongoing

We wish we could say that our relationship has been conflict-free since that rocky first year. After all, we help lead a church here in Michigan; Dave serves as chaplain for the Detroit Lions; and we speak all around the country on how to build a lasting marriage. Shouldn't we have a perfect marriage by now?

This may not be a very good question to ask, but if we were to ask it, the answer would definitely be a no. Even as we've matured together, we have never grown out of the fact that we are both passionate individuals—and why would we want to grow out of this? Our passion is a huge part of who we are as individuals.

Lobotomizing one's personality in order to avoid the conflict that arises from it will also remove the very parts of that personality that make them capable of the good things they are uniquely created to experience. So yes, we are both passionate, which means we still bump heads a lot. Yes, after more than three decades of marriage, we still get into arguments.

But the real truth about marriage is this: marriage is indeed glorious, and it is indeed difficult. You love your spouse, but you also can't stand your spouse at times. And this seemingly unromantic reality should not be hidden below deck with the gunpowder—just waiting to ignite and send the marriage plummeting to the depths. It should be talked about from day one. Otherwise, many couples think that if they are experiencing conflict, something is wrong with their marriage.

The truth is that *conflict is normal*—and when we start learning how to resolve conflict together, we actually grow closer to one another and more intimate in our marriage. God can actually use our conflicts to make us one.

When you talk with couples who have been married for forty years, fifty years, or even more, you begin to note common themes. They will tell you they experience difficulties like any other couple, but they work through them. They don't quit. They keep on working toward peace with one another (see Hebrews 12:14). And as a result, they experience God's perfect grace in their less-than-perfect lifetime together.

Over the next few chapters, we will share several proven strategies for resolving conflict in marriage. God has used these strategies to help us weather our own storms through the years so that even when we took on water, we never sank into the abyss.

No matter what conflicts you have experienced, are experiencing, or will experience in marriage, you will find that God's Word is helpful and practical—full of hope, yet not always easy to apply. We pray that these principles for resolving conflict will help you thrive in the most important relationship in your life.

Six

Welcome to the Jungle

One Saturday several years ago, we flew to Illinois to watch one of our sons play in a college football game. As I (Dave) drove our rental car from the Chicago airport to the stadium, I glanced over at Ann, who was napping. I thought to myself, *I am so lucky to be married to this woman.* I took note of the cute little lines on her beautiful face and reminisced about all the memories we had shared over the years. In that moment, I was filled with love for her all over again.

And so it only makes sense that after this moving moment of reflection and gratitude I would demonstrate these feelings to her. So how did I behave for the rest of the day with my beloved wife, the love of my life?

Well, in a few words, I was a jerk.

I belittled her for not being the great navigator that we all know the person in the passenger seat is supposed to be. I rolled my eyes at her. Made her feel like she was stupid. And somehow, I was oblivious to the way I was treating her. I thought it was a good day all around—until, that is, we were hurriedly driving back to the airport after the game. She hadn't said much for most of the day, but that was about to change.

"I just need to say this," she huffed. "I am so tired of you treating me like I'm the biggest idiot in the world! It's like I can't do anything right! You have been a jerk to me all day!"

"What! Are you kidding me? The only jerk in this car is you!"

This is always a great approach to building oneness in your marriage.

How dare she say such a thing to me, especially at the moment I was racing to get us back to the airport on time! "What are you talking about? Look, Mrs. Navigator, can you just pay attention to the GPS and help me out here?"

Ah, the irony—we were going to be speaking together on the topic of marriage at church the next day.

We were both still mad and not really talking to each other as we boarded the plane. There was a young couple sitting across the aisle from us who were all over each other like newly-weds. I saw Ann glance over at them with a look of admiration and a longing for our relationship to be that tender. I looked at them and thought, *Obviously they aren't married yet.*

The Selfishness Problem

If this conflict had occurred in our first year of marriage, such a fight would have escalated into a screaming match. The conflict would have gone unresolved, and we would have stuffed our bitterness deep inside.

But after more than thirty years of practice, we had learned a lot about how to defuse and then resolve these arguments. One of our most important principles for attaining resolution is found in Matthew 7:3–5: "Why do you look at the speck of sawdust in your brother's eye and pay no attention to the plank in your own eye? How can you say to your brother, 'Let me take the speck out of your eye,' when all the time there is a plank in your own eye? You hypocrite, first take the plank out of your own eye, and then you will see clearly to remove the speck from your brother's eye."

Translation? In any conflict, you've got to stop and seek understanding about what *you* did to spark the problem.

In this case, I eventually settled down and realized I *had* treated Ann like dirt that day. I was knee-deep in selfishness, which by definition is generally something that oneself has a hard time recognizing. It's like when you're swimming in the ocean and the undertow slowly inches you down the shoreline—you usually don't realize how far you've moved while you're still in the water. In fact, if your spouse is sitting near you right now, I want you to look over at him or her.

You are currently looking at the second most selfish person on the planet!

It's almost impossible to identify selfishness in the moment it is first happening. One of the best things about a vertical viewpoint is that it brings Someone into the mix who specializes in the impossible, beckoning us to follow him to places that are humanly impossible. One of those places is into a life lived above and away from the selfishness that resides within each of us.

The apostle Paul demonstrates this invitation into the seemingly impossible in his letter to the Philippians: "Do nothing from selfishness or empty conceit, but with humility of mind regard one another as more important than yourselves; do not merely look out for your own personal interests, but also for the interests of others" (Philippians 2:3–4 NASB).

When we apply this passage to the conflicts we experience with others, its meaning becomes nothing less than profound. For most people, becoming aware of one's selfishness in the middle of a conflict cannot happen. There is too much anger.

Too much emotion. It's a good thing that when we connect vertically with God and bring him into our relationships, he grants us strength and ability higher than our horizontal humanity. Selfishness can never be conquered on our own. We simply do not have the power. We have to ask Jesus for *his* resurrection power—he regularly raises dead things to life.

Trust me, our selfishness will kill us and our marriages, so it's time to ask for some serious divine power.

In the middle of your conflicts, begin listening for the whisper within that reminds you to pull back, examine yourself and not just your spouse (even if they have fault in the matter as well), and come to grips with your own selfishness and conceit. Rather than blaming your spouse, humble yourself and consider your spouse's needs to be more important than your own. Being willing to lean into the vertical truth of Philippians 2:3–4 will be a game-changer for the selfishness problem.

You Are in a War

You are in a war. We know what you're thinking: *Yeah, I know! She is the enemy, and I'm going to take her down!* Or *He's the enemy; he doesn't even love me!* We hear you. It often feels like your spouse is the enemy, but the truth is, this couldn't be further from the truth.

There is something else going on in your marriage that you can't even see with your physical eyes. In fact, Paul talks about it in his letter to the Ephesians: "For our struggle is not against flesh and blood, but against the rulers, against the authorities, against the powers of this dark world and against the spiritual forces of evil in the heavenly realms" (6:12).

Once again, it seems that we like to apply verses like this one to *anything* in our lives, churches, or work situations—*anything* other than relationships or marriages. But this verse and many others like it are full of theology about relationships. God says that your war is *not* against your wife or your husband. It's not against flesh and blood. It's not against another human being. It's not even against yourself.

Okay, then what is it against? Rulers, authorities, and powers of the dark world. It is against spiritual forces of evil in the heavenly realms. It's against an enemy—a spiritual ruler and authority in a spiritual realm that you can't even see with your physical eyes.

God created the universe. He also created angels before he created human beings. The first of the angels to rebel was Satan, who because of his desire to usurp God and take his position was thrown out of heaven, along with others who followed his lead. Jesus himself noted about Satan, "The thief comes only to steal and kill and destroy; I have come that they may have life, and have it to the full" (John 10:10).

With this verse, Jesus basically says, "I want to give you the greatest relationship you've ever dreamed of. I have an unbelievable plan for your marriage and for your relationship. But the thief, Satan, wants to steal and kill and destroy your relationship."

There is a war going on, and your marriage is on the front lines. Even so, many of us tend to think that good marriages and relationships are being experienced on some distant romantic balcony, not on a spiritual battlefield.

I've Married the Wrong Person!

If you're like us, you don't normally wake up every day tuned into the reality that your marriage is a spiritual battlefield. Instead, you wake up thinking, *Is she going to make me happy today? Is he going to meet my needs?* And when your spouse doesn't fulfill these expectations, you think, *Maybe I married the wrong person!*

I once promoted an upcoming marriage series at my church by saying, "Next week's sermon is called 'Now That You've Married the Wrong Person.'" Droves of people approached me and said they couldn't wait for this sermon. "Why?" I asked. In their own unique ways, they all said they had indeed married the wrong people.

We've all felt that way at some point.

The truth is that by purely "horizontal" standards of just being human, everyone marries the wrong person. We mean that if you expect a human to fulfill a Spirit-sized hole in your life, then no matter how generous, understanding, sexually charged, or even spiritual the other person may be, they cannot meet those expectations. Ever.

But the wrong person can become the right person when they are not expected to do for you what only God can do.

This perception is a part of being aware of the war. It is doubtful that any of our brave soldiers in Iraq or Afghanistan are waking up on the front lines today and thinking to themselves, *Am I going to be happy today? Who's going to get me my coffee? I sure hope my fellow soldier meets my needs today.*

We're not saying that happiness is not a wonderful thing to think about, but these guys are waking up in a battle situation, putting on their helmets, loading their weapons, and saying, "What's our mission today? Where is the enemy? What's his strategy? Let's move out!" Why? Because they understand they are in a war.

If you will wake up every day knowing there is a real enemy who hates you and hates the possibility that you will "do marriage" God's way—and who has his sights on you because he wants to destroy your marriage and your legacy—well, then, that reality changes everything. It's no longer about my selfish desire just to be happy; it becomes about God's bigger plan of showing himself to the world through your marriage.

That's epic.

We first heard this truth two weeks before we were married. We attended a marriage conference we now are privileged to speak at—FamilyLife's Weekend to Remember. They taught us that there's an enemy of our marriage who wants to take us down because he wants to stop God's plan for our marriage. That plan is for oneness, and this oneness will produce glory back to him.

But Satan also has a plan for our marriages, and it's summed up in one word: *divorce*.

Fighting the Real Enemy

The word *divorce* and the real fight to avoid it are serious enough business that we want to collectively address it as "us" again. Three months into our marriage, we were in Casper, Wyoming, visiting Ann's aunt and uncle. Her aunt and uncle were both at work, so we were alone in the house—which should have led to good things happening. Instead, we got into a pretty good fight.

It became very heated with lots of screaming and yelling. Finally, Dave did what Dave used to always do. He left the bedroom and said, "I'm outta here. I can't stand you! I don't want to be in the same room with you!"

Ann was furious, but she remembered what we had been taught those few weeks before. As Dave walked out of the room, she yelled, "Why are we fighting each other when we should be fighting the enemy?"

Dave was a couple of steps into the hallway when she said it, and it made him mad, but in a different sort of way than before. It made him mad because he knew she was right. He didn't want to admit it, but he turned around and went back into the room with her. This one statement reminded us that we were indeed in a war, just not against one another. We decided (that time, at least) to fight the real enemy instead.

But this drama plays out in everyday marriage. We tend to forget the real truth that matters most. We get so hurt that our natural tendency is to hurt the other person in return, and so we start shooting our spouse over the little things instead of attacking the deeper issues. And above all, we forget who the real enemy is.

If you can picture this from sort of a cosmic spiritual realm, just imagine Satan looking at Dave and Ann from a foxhole across the battlefield. He sees us turning toward each other with guns a-blazin'. No doubt he's just sitting there smirking, saying, "This is easy. I don't have to do anything because they're shooting each other! They don't even realize their real enemy is out here!"

Jesus told his followers that the evidence proving they were his followers would be found in the way they loved one another (see John 13:35). Satan has no doubt heard this message as well, so his tactic is simple: "I will destroy all of that in relationships!" And if you consider that one of the first things God did in creation was to institute the relationship of marriage, we can see why there is a special target on the backs of married couples.

You Will Be Wounded

In a war, people get hurt. In marriage and relationships, people get wounded. It may not sound like great news, but the realization of this reality is actually a gift. We should expect it instead of being surprised by it when it happens.

The Amplified Bible's translation of Ephesians 5:33 offers a fascinating glimpse into the way husbands and wives should consider one another:

> However, each man among you [without exception] is to love his wife as his very own self [with behavior worthy of respect and esteem, always seeking the best for her with an attitude of lovingkindness], and the wife [must see to it] that she respects *and* delights in her husband [that she notices him and prefers him and treats him with loving concern, treasuring him, honoring him, and holding him dear].

Lovingkindness. Respect. Delight. Preferring. Treasuring. Holding dear. There's a part of us that longs for our spouse to hear these words from Scripture so that *they* will change and start doing them. It is so easy to focus on our spouse and what they are not doing in the marriage to satisfy us. At our core, we are selfish and believe that we deserve to have our needs met at all times by our spouse. But guess what? Your spouse is thinking the same thing about you! And here's another news flash: both of you will be let down in some way by each other. No one can meet all of our needs. The minute we realize this truth is the minute we can finally begin looking instead to the only One who can and will meet those needs—if we let him.

When we go to a marriage retreat or read a marriage book together, we begin to think, *He's going to love me better now*, or *She's going to respect me now.* Prepare yourself for the very possibility that he or she won't. Yes, we hope these experiences have been helpful and you will both understand marriage and each other better than before. But again, if you think that *they* are finally going to completely give you what you need, you'll be hurt, frustrated, and bitter . . . because they were *never* made to fill you. Even at their best, your expectations need to be appropriately tempered. Because only God can fill you.

Seven

THE SHAPES OF
Wrath

I (Dave) will never forget the day when Ann approached me in the kitchen and began critiquing me about something in our relationship. At that point, we had been married for about five years. She meant to be constructive—that is, she really wanted to help me—but she had not yet learned how to do it without hurting my feelings. I felt belittled, which rarely leads to any good place for men or women.

This feeling was like a fuse, and it only took a few minutes before the rest of me exploded in anger.

What happened next remains clear in my mind, because this particular day was one of those turning points in our relationship. Ann was very disappointed. "Every time I bring something up, you get mad," she said. "So just forget it. Why waste my time? You just blow up."

As she turned to walk away, I screamed after her, "I do not! What are you even talking about?"

She gestured toward me as if she were a prosecutor pleading her case before a judge. "There you have it—exhibit A! Thank you. I rest my case."

Checking under the Hood

We all get angry at times—it's part of being human. The problem is that we often don't recognize or comprehend the roots of our anger, so we don't know how to handle it when it comes. If you are driving a car and you notice steam or smoke billowing out of the engine compartment, you can't simply continue driving; you must pull over immediately and check under the hood to see if your engine is overheating, or worse.

An argument, like smoke billowing out of a car, is often a symptom of a deeper issue—not always, but often. And especially if there is serious "heat" in an argument regarding a particular topic or discussion point, wisdom says that you should pull the argument over and check under the hood to determine what the real problem is. So when anger pops up in conflict—as it almost always does—you need to check under the hood and ask yourself, "What's *causing* that anger?"

For the first time in my life, the hood had been raised, and I could see at least a little of the real problem. My angry words had been bouncing around the kitchen like bullets ricocheting off concrete—and even though Ann was my best friend, my words were far from friendly fire. They were downright mean.

Deep down inside, I knew she was right, but I just couldn't admit it to her yet.

But that particular argument did lead me to begin checking more often under the hood to try to determine what was going on. Why was I so angry all the time?

A few days later, I was meeting with the three men who, to this day, I call my personal accountability group. Once every week, the four of us get together to talk about our lives and deal with the nitty-gritty of being husbands, dads, and brothers in a fallen world. These guys know everything about me.

I asked them, "Of all the emotions you experience as a man, which one do you feel most often?"

They looked at me like I was suddenly wearing a pink dress and high heels. "Emotions? What on earth are you talking about?" They knew what I meant, but they enjoyed giving me a hard time.

"You know, emotions—like joy, happiness, sadness, anger, frustration? Which one?"

In a heartbeat, they responded in unison: "That's easy—anger!"

So I told them about the kitchen incident a few days earlier and my habitual pattern of lashing out in anger whenever I experienced conflict with Ann. "I need to find out where this anger is coming from," I said. This conversation raised the hood just a bit more, because for the first time, I was willing to invite someone else to look under there as well.

Defaulting to Anger

I began to study anger, and I learned that psychologists call it a "second emotion." This means that anger is not usually the first emotion we feel in a stressful situation. The first emotion may be hurt, frustration, fear, or something else—but we instead jump to anger because we're too uncomfortable with the initial emotion. In that kitchen argument with Ann, I was feeling hurt, but I didn't know how to admit it. So I let myself immediately default to anger instead. I honestly had no idea that I flipped to that second emotion all the time.

But everyone else realized it—and especially Ann.

Other examples of my "default anger" began surfacing. I was trying to fix a dryer, and my four-year-old son, CJ, asked what I was doing. He was already showing signs that he was mechanically inclined, so I asked if he wanted to help.

"Sure!" he said.

I thought this experience would go well, but as it turned out, he was too young and not yet strong enough to turn his tiny screwdriver. Despite his best efforts, his little fingers kept slipping and fumbling. I was in a hurry, and in my frustration, I blasted him.

"CJ, just turn it!"

There was such hurt on his little face that all he could do was get up and leave. He didn't want to be yelled at. I had blown it again.

But this incident happened right at the time I was beginning to study anger and its power in my life. It was an "aha!" moment for me. I realized that I had behaved like a complete idiot—you can't expect a four-year-old to handle a screwdriver as adeptly as a grown man.

Oh no! I thought. *Do I really want to be* that *dad who pushes away his own son with anger?* I had a lot of work to do, but I was beginning to embrace it.

I also learned about different types of anger. *Situation-specific anger* is related directly to the situation or circumstances that spark it. Usually, this type of anger is easier to control, and, in fact, it can sometimes even be constructive. For example, one might feel righteous indignation at an injustice or when one witnesses cruelty. This is the righteous anger that motivated William Wilberforce to courageously work to end the slave trade. It also motivated Jesus to drive the money changers out of the temple (see John 2).

Another type is *displaced anger.* This anger is misdirected toward the wrong target. When one is angry over a situation at work and comes home, only to yell at a child for spilling milk at the dinner table, that's displaced anger. Anytime a road-raging driver begins tailgating me, flashing his headlights and honking to try to pass me, I really wish I could sit down with the guy and say, "You've got displaced anger, dude. What's your real problem? Here, let me help you look under the hood."

That would probably not turn out well.

The ABCs of Handling Anger

For situation-specific or displaced anger, I've learned what I call the "ABCs of Handling Anger."

A: ACKNOWLEDGE AND ADMIT YOUR ANGER

Paul tells the Ephesians, "'In your anger do not sin': Do not let the sun go down while you are still angry" (4:26). This verse implies that anger is a natural, God-given emotion. Why else would it say, "In your anger"? Everyone will deal with anger at some point, but this doesn't necessarily mean we have to sin—or miss the mark—because of it. So plan to deal with it, but better yet, plan to deal with it *now*. Get over it quickly. Don't let it fester inside.

Unfortunately, many Christians find it very difficult to admit when they are angry. They think anger is always a sin. I remember sitting in a meeting with the elders of our church. The guy sitting next to me was obviously becoming more and more angry over the situation we were discussing. I leaned over and whispered, "Hey, dude, you're getting a little hot, huh?"

"No, not me," he replied.

"Yeah, you are." I could tell he didn't want to admit it.

"What makes you think I'm angry?"

"Because there's fire coming out of your nostrils!" I laughed. And yet he still kept denying it.

Anger is not a sin, but if we don't acknowledge it early, it can certainly lead to sin. God knows every thought and emotion we have, so why hide them? Be honest about those moments when you're angry with your spouse. The second we finally admit we're angry is the second we finally start moving toward getting a grip on this anger. This honesty will put us miles ahead in the process of finding resolution and peace.

B: BACKTRACK TO THE FIRST EMOTION

This one is huge because it is so easy to go around and around in a moment of heated discussion and literally get lost in your own argument, forgetting what the initial issue was in the first place.

So go back to the root cause of your anger and find the emotion you skipped over in favor of anger instead. Was it fear? Sadness? Hurt? In my own marriage, I usually skip over hurt and take the fast lane right to anger.

I have realized that I just don't do emotional pain very well. In fact, I don't know many guys who do. I believe that women are much better with this emotion. Have you ever come home to find your wife in tears on the couch? You ask her why, and she says she has just had the hardest day and that the kids were mean to her.

Now flip the coin. Women, have you ever found your husband sitting on the couch in tears because someone hurt him emotionally at work? Probably not. Instead, he just reacts in anger toward you all night and you don't know why . . . and neither does he. Well, now you know.

Usually when I teach this practice of "backtracking to the first emotion," I wrap an extension cord around my waist with the plug hanging on the floor. I then try to backtrack down the cord to find out what it's plugged into. *That* emotion of hurt or frustration is what I really need to deal with rather than just exploding in anger. Once I know what that emotion is, *then* I can actually do something about it.

I need to be honest with myself and admit that I'm hurt and that I'm not comfortable with that emotion. Then I need to be honest with my wife. "Honey, that hurt me. What you said made me feel devalued as a man. That's why I lashed out." Now we can truly communicate.

This is where communication starts. I listen. My wife listens. And together, we start making headway in our conflict. For most of us, it's not fun to go there, but trust me, it works.

C: CONFESS YOUR ANGER APPROPRIATELY

There are appropriate and inappropriate ways to confess your anger. Confessing appropriately means coming clean about your emotions and mistakes with honesty, gentleness, and self-control.

I remember a day when I picked up our boys from gymnastics practice. Ann normally picked everyone up, but on this particular day, I was the chauffeur.

When my young son CJ saw me instead of his mom, his first words—in front of the other parents, mind you—were, "Oh, it's you, Dad. I thought Mom was coming."

I cringed at his obvious disappointment, but I tried to mask it. As we were walking out, I was talking with a mom from our church when CJ began tugging at my pants, asking me—well, more like badgering me—to buy him a snack from the vending machine.

Still reeling from his initial greeting, I snapped at him, "CJ, just hold on. I'm talking."

"But, Dad, I want something."

"Just hold on!" I said in that loud-yet-still-quiet-enough-to-remain-unembarrassed sort of way that most parents have mastered.

"But Mom always gets me something!"

Inside, I had run out of patience. I reached down and squeezed his arm to get his attention, but I didn't realize how angry I was—and I squeezed his arm too hard. He screamed out in pain. I mean, *really* screamed. In front of all those parents. I could just hear them thinking, *Isn't that Reverend Wilson? Should we call Child Protective Services, or at least just leave his church and tell everyone why?*

It was not my finest hour. On the drive home, I came to my senses and went through the ABCs in my head as I drove. You can do it that quickly. I admitted my anger, backtracked to the hurt that sparked my anger, and realized that I needed to confess my anger to my sons.

"Boys," I said, "back there at the gymnastics center, did you think I was mad?"

Wide-eyed, they nodded yes in unison. (Side note: the kids see *everything*.)

"Do you know why Dad was angry?"

CJ piped up. "Yeah, I didn't interrupt you properly."

He assumed the fault was all his, which is what we teach our children to do—mainly because we as parents have such a hard time being honest with our children about our own faults in the process. I decided that I needed to address my mistake, not just let it be eclipsed by their childlike innocence—which I knew might do the trick this time, but wouldn't last forever.

"CJ, you wanted Mom to pick you up instead of me. You're seven years old, and of course you wanted your mom. But it hurt my feelings, and I took it out on you. Guys, Dad was wrong. I'm sorry. I shouldn't have squeezed your arm so hard, CJ. That anger was inappropriate. Will you forgive me?"

Before my confession was even finished, CJ replied, "Oh yeah!" (Side note: kids are usually quick to forgive.)

That was an incredible moment with my sons, but the best

part of the story is that twenty minutes later, when I walked into the house, Ann got a husband who was no longer carrying displaced anger that would have ended up being directed at her.

Gaining control of our anger is critically important. If we don't get back to the source, we will continue to carry that fire into our marriage, most definitely hurting the ones whom we love the most. They deserve better than this from us.

Anger That Runs Deep

The ABCs seem to really help with moments of situational and displaced anger, but they're not as effective with the third type: *chronic anger.* Chronic anger runs deep. It's similar to displaced anger in that it originates from somewhere else, but it generally goes much further. It is often buried deep under layers of hurt, anger, and bitterness that go back many years.

Chronically angry people can explode anywhere, anytime. You never know what will set them off. This sort of anger is a buried land mine just waiting for someone to step on it— deeply buried, yet shallowly accessible. And when it blows up, everyone—usually even the angry person—is generally shocked.

"Where did *that* come from?"

This was my story during the first twenty years of our marriage. I suffered from chronic anger for years and never knew it.

When we were very young, my father left me and my four siblings. He was an airline pilot, and he had been unfaithful to my mother on many occasions. As expected, my mother finally had enough, and their marriage ended.

As you can imagine, when he tried to connect with us kids, I pushed him away. Even when I was a young man in college, the issues were still unresolved. I have vivid memories of his attempts to attend my football games. Even after all those years,

I wanted nothing to do with him. I told him to his face that he didn't get to be part of my life because he had walked out on us.

Like many other men with similar backgrounds, I had no idea how all of this buried hurt and rejection had wounded me as a boy, as an adolescent, and as a young man. I was deeply bitter and angry, and I unknowingly brought that chronic anger into my marriage.

Choosing to Forgive

When I was in my late twenties, I remember sitting with Ann as we watched our young boys play on the floor. I said to her, "Can you believe that my dad left me when I was only their age?"

Ann looked at me with gentleness and love—and she had the courage to lovingly confront me. "You know you have issues with your dad, don't you?"

Naturally, I became defensive and abrasive. "What are you talking about? I don't have any issues with that! I forgave him years ago."

She remained my safe place, even while I was rejecting it. "Do you know what you're like when your dad calls? You hold the phone ten inches away from your ear. You look miserable. You talk as little as possible. You don't even engage in the relationship. You merely tolerate it."

And then she dropped the bomb. "I think you need to forgive your dad."

Talk about ruining a relaxing Sunday afternoon! We were having a great time, and then she ruined it with what every man hates—unsolicited free advice.

But of course she was right. God has blessed me with a woman who knows me through and through and has the discernment to know when something is wrong.

Later that night, I was still churning inside. I asked God, "Were you trying to tell me something today through Ann?"

I think he was almost rolling his divine eyes as he gently responded to my heart, "Yes."

"Okay," I responded, "I'll call him next Sunday."

The next day, a friend told me I needed to read a book he had just finished—*Forgive and Forget* by Lewis Smedes. He said he had thought about me as he was reading it. Hmm, it was almost as if everyone who knew me well and cared about me already knew about my issues of unforgiveness with my dad. How had I missed it? That really didn't matter—God's gift to help me miss it no more was being offered through the loving honesty of my wife and real friends.

I read that book several times—and it literally changed my life. One quote in particular had a profound impact on me. "Forgiving," Smedes wrote, is to "set a prisoner free, but you discover that the real prisoner was yourself."* This was a perfect description of my life. I was imprisoned by twenty years of bitterness, resentment, and chronic anger.

I would love to tell you that those moments of discovery led to an instant resolution of the matter, but the truth is, it took me four years to finally and fully forgive my dad. That's how long it took for God to restore my heart—and he continued to do it through the wisdom of his Word, the working of his Spirit, and the willingness of his people to "intrude" into my life with love and truth. It was a hurt I had held in my clenched fist for more than thirty years, but God slowly opened my hands and my heart to forgive.

After this process, the Detroit Lions had a road trip to Tampa, where my dad lived. As chaplain for the Lions, I flew

---

* Lewis B. Smedes, *Forgive and Forget: Healing the Hurts We Don't Deserve* (1984; repr., San Francisco: HarperSanFrancisco, 1996), 133.

down with the team and invited my dad to stay in the team hotel the night before the game. The next day, we drove to the stadium in his car, and I finally said what I needed to say. "Dad, I've got to tell you something. I can't remember ever saying this to you. I love you . . . and I forgive you."

Time seemed to stand still.

The car filled with dead silence as I searched his face for a response. He looked puzzled. He didn't even know what I was forgiving him for. Isn't that both tragic and amazing? But finally he muttered, "Thank you, and . . . I love you too."

I was thirty-two years old, and I had just heard my dad say "I love you" for the very first time. I often say I became a man at age thirty-two—and it didn't happen until I forgave my father as Christ had forgiven me. This process finally broke me free from the chronic anger I had held on to for years. All those years, I had thought I had locked my dad out of my life, but I was the one who was locked up. The day I forgave my dad was the day I became free to become the husband, father, and man God had created me to be.

Several years later, I officiated at my dad's funeral. As I stood and looked at his casket, I was so grateful that God had done spiritual surgery on my heart. I was free, and I actually felt a love for this man toward whom I had harbored bitterness for decades.

The process of confronting and healing deep anger requires time, commitment, help from qualified counselors, and a willingness to trust and follow God. Thank God that he has set me free from chronic anger—and he can do the same for you.

Eight

Just Zip It

I (Dave) remember walking into the kitchen one evening. Ann began telling me how hard her day had been. The kids had been out of control and disobedient. I had been gone all day and the house was a mess. Her schedule was chaotic . . . and so forth and so on. I stopped her midsentence and told her I would be right back. I ran upstairs to my office for a few moments and then came back with a note for her to read, something I really thought could help her.

She looked pleased and excited when I handed her what I had written down just for her. She actually thought it was a letter of how much I loved and appreciated all that she did for our family. But as she read the opening sentence out loud, her smile quickly became a scowl. It read, "10 Things That Will Help You Get More Organized . . . #1: Begin each day with a written plan."

Yes, I actually wrote that. You can imagine how *that* moment ended.

I was so naive—or should I say, stupid—to think that this is what Ann really wanted from me: to help fix her problem. How could I be so dumb? She literally tore up that note and threw it back in my face. I actually yelled, "Those tips were from God. I prayed first before writing those down for you!" Needless to say, she knew better than I did exactly where those tips came from—and it wasn't from God. It was from a husband who had no idea that his wife just wanted her man to shut up and listen.

When we zip our lips long enough to truly listen to what our spouse is saying, we can actually begin to hear what is being said behind the words.

Two Ears and One Mouth

In his letter, James tells us, "My dear brothers and sisters, take note of this: Everyone should be quick to listen, slow to speak and slow to become angry" (1:19). If you've ever heard two people arguing, you know how revolutionary these words are. When we are engaged in a conflict, we usually exhibit the exact opposite qualities—we become *slow to listen*, *quick to speak*, and *quick to become angry*.

Though it's been pointed out before, I'll say it again: we have two ears and one mouth. Remembering this ratio can revolutionize moments of conflict—if we will listen twice as much as we speak. But instead, we are more prone to think only about our own arguments, our own planned comebacks, and our own rebuttals.

In fact, the biblical command to be "slow to speak" is especially important for those with strong verbal skills. Just because you *can* outtalk your spouse in an argument doesn't mean you *should*. Being the last one verbally standing does not mean you are the one who is right. You can be the smartest person in the room, yet also the most foolish. Maybe that's why Proverbs 18:2 reads, "Fools find no pleasure in understanding but delight in airing their own opinions."

There's another way to paraphrase the message of James 1:19. Are you ready? Here it is: *Shut up . . . and listen!*

This advice may not sound very touchy-feely, but it is very helpful and highly effective. It leads me to recognize those moments when I need to turn off my phone, turn off my laptop, and turn off the TV so I can *actually* look my wife in the eyes and *actually* listen to what she has to say. When I really listen on this level, I usually learn that there's something deeper she's trying to communicate. She may not be saying it perfectly, and she may even be saying it in anger. But if I truly listen and ask God to give me understanding and discernment, I can usually discover the real root of the issue.

As a young husband, I actually had to learn (again, the hard way) how to shut up. I have a tendency to think that when Ann is sharing a problem or struggle, her real desire is for me to fix it for her. (I think a lot of us men think this way.)

Remember the story of our tenth anniversary? Remember how God told me to shut up and listen? Our tenth anniversary was when God showed me how messed up my priorities had become. And sadly, that wasn't the first time we had argued about my priorities. For *years*, I had never really heard her. When she said, "You're never home . . . I feel like I'm raising the boys alone," I felt like she was needy and didn't appreciate what I was doing. Didn't I need to work and provide for my family? Why didn't she appreciate that?

Can you see how my own arguments and conclusions were drowning out her words? But when I shut up and listened to her, I began to discern what she was really saying. And believe me, I felt so stupid that I couldn't hear it for all those years.

She was saying, "I don't feel like I'm a priority in your life," which made her feel unloved. She was responding out of hurt and anger by not showing respect for me, and eventually, the hurt was so bad that she shut down, losing her feelings for me. We were caught in what Emerson Eggerichs calls the "Crazy

Cycle." As he writes in his book *Love and Respect*, a woman's number one need is to feel cherished and loved, and a man's number one need is to feel respected.* If a wife doesn't feel loved by her husband, she reacts by not showing respect for him. Then he responds to that lack of respect by not loving her.

Ann and I were caught in that vicious cycle and couldn't break out until I finally began to shut up and listen.

Of course, there can't be any true conversation or communion without both listening and speaking in a give-and-take way. We already know we need to be "slow to speak." But when the time comes to speak, what do we say?

Speak the Truth in Love

The apostle Paul writes, "Instead, speaking the truth in love, we will grow to become in every respect the mature body of him who is the head, that is, Christ" (Ephesians 4:15). This passage tells us that learning to speak the truth in love is an important part of maturing to be like Jesus Christ. And there's no better way to practice this discipline than in the closest of all relationships: marriage.

We often skip over this significant truth, choosing instead to displace it with other things that we somehow assume will ultimately foster maturity in its place. Attend church every week. Read the Bible and pray every day. Join a small group. Of course, as a pastor, I'm in support of every single one of these disciplines. They are good, and they are good for you. However, they cannot take the place of learning to speak the truth in love as a pathway to spiritual and relational maturity.

Learning to balance truth and love is a lifelong learning

---

* Emerson Eggerichs, *Love and Respect: The Love She Most Desires, the Respect He Desperately Needs* (Nashville: Nelson, 2004), 6.

process. On the one hand, some of us are hardwired as "lovers." Lovers often have a hard time speaking difficult truth to others, mainly because they don't want to hurt them. On the other hand, some of us are hardwired as "truth-tellers." Truth-tellers feel like they have a mandate from God above to tell everybody the truth, even people they don't know or who don't care to hear it.

Regardless of the default tendencies of your personality, if you want to resolve conflict in marriage (or in any relationship), at some point you must talk through the cause of that conflict. This will involve speaking the truth. However, if that truth is not packaged well, it will probably not be received well.

But when it's wrapped in love, your spouse can more easily hear it.

Over the years, we've had more than our share of conflicts that revealed truth, but that truth has often surfaced like an explosion, hurled in a spirit of anger, frustration, and even vengeance. We've screamed at each other. We've hurled sarcasm at each other. And you know what?

It never works!

When we try to speak truth into a situation, there is a huge temptation to be one-sided and to only see things our way. All married couples suffer from "selective vision"—we can't seem to see our own faults, no matter how large they may be. But we can easily see our spouse's shortcomings, no matter how small they may be.

So how do we speak the truth in love? Here are a few scriptural suggestions.

1. Focus on encouraging your spouse rather than attacking. If your goal is to pin your spouse to the mat and force them to admit what they've done wrong, you won't make it very far. Such intentions and actions are the opposite of speaking the truth in love.

The apostle Paul reminds us to "encourage one another and build one another up" (1 Thessalonians 5:11 ESV). It is hard to encourage someone when you are only focusing on the worst components of their personality or habits. You end up seeing only what you are looking for instead of seeing them fully. Try taking note of what your spouse is doing right and how they are maturing. Speak life into them. Appeal not only to the woman or man they are now, but also to the woman or man they are becoming.

2. Give your spouse grace. The apostle Paul also writes, "Let your speech always be gracious" (Colossians 4:6 ESV). Be merciful and compassionate, even when your spouse is in the wrong. Show the type of grace to your spouse that God is constantly showing you. This is the essence of the gospel, which also means it is the key to strength and longevity in all relationships, including marriage.

3. Apply the "love chapter" to your speech. The famous letter of the apostle Paul to the Corinthians describes what love really looks like: "Love is patient and kind; love does not envy or boast; it is not arrogant or rude. It does not insist on its own way; it is not irritable or resentful; it does not rejoice at wrongdoing, but rejoices with the truth. Love bears all things, believes all things, hopes all things, endures all things. Love never ends" (1 Corinthians 13:4–8 ESV).

It is all too easy to let these familiar words run right over us. We love the beauty of the way they sound during a wedding ceremony, but they often end up meaning very little to us practically. Instead of only admiring them, try applying these descriptions to your actual conversations.

When I talk with my spouse, am I patient and kind? Do I become envious? Do I boast that my way is right, even to the point of becoming arrogant or rude? Am I irritable or resentful, even finding reasons to rejoice at my spouse's wrongdoing because it gives me the upper hand? Or do I rejoice in the truth instead? Do I truly endeavor in my marriage to bear all things, believe all things, hope all things, and endure all things? When I speak with my spouse, do they know that my love for them is like God's love for me: never-ending?

Writer Shaunti Feldhahn discovered in her research that "one reason the highly happy couples are so happy is that they value kindness rather than telling it like it is. Instead of letting their conversations be seasoned with brutal honesty, these couples choose to follow the apostle Paul's advice to the church in the ancient city of Colossae—to 'let your conversation be always full of grace.' They understand the power of words to destroy and that nowhere is this power to be more in control than in the relationships that matter to us most." *

Remember that your relationship is more important than winning the argument. If you speak the truth in love during a conflict, at some point you will need to tell your spouse some things that are difficult to hear. But if your speech is seasoned with encouragement, grace, and love, your words will have the mature and constructive impact you truly desire them to have.

Iron Sharpens Iron

Of course, the flip side to *speaking* the truth is *hearing* the truth. Truth works best when it is welcomed. And yes, I know—the truth is so hard to hear sometimes.

In *Creativity, Inc.*, Ed Catmull, the president of Pixar, describes the history of the company and details the process

---

* Shaunti Feldhahn, *The Surprising Secrets of Highly Happy Marriages: The Little Things That Make a Big Difference* (Colorado Springs: Multnomah, 2013), 165–66.

behind its incredible string of hit films. Early in the process of production, Catmull says, each of their hit movies was terrible. But they built a development method in which each film was picked apart by what they dubbed the Braintrust—a group of experienced Pixar colleagues who critiqued the work with total candor. It was difficult to hear at times, but this level of total, unbridled honesty helped to mold these films into the incredible works of art they would eventually become.*

When I first read about that process, I thought about my own life. I realized I was in a bad movie—and so is every one of us. We're sinners . . . broken and separated from God. If we won't let someone come in and offer us total candor—if we refuse to hear them speak the truth to us in love—then we'll never mature; we'll never experience all that God so graciously desires for us during our time on this planet.

The power of lovingly honest candor is the essence of the truth found in Proverbs: "As iron sharpens iron, so one person sharpens another" (27:17). Nowhere does this principle ring truer than in the relational realities of marriage. God uses your spouse to sharpen you—to help you grow and mature. If you never see and accept the truth—that is, if you never allow yourself to hear it from your spouse and instead always choose to shut down and get defensive—then you will never see the fullness of what God can do in your life.

But if you will have the courage to listen to truth, you will grow to understand what you need to work on changing and what needs to be entrusted to God to change. As you are willingly sharpened by the spouse Christ gave you, you will actually

---

* Ed Catmull, *Creativity, Inc.: Overcoming the Unseen Forces That Stand in the Way of True Inspiration* (New York: Random House, 2014); see Ed Catmull, "Inside the Pixar Braintrust," *Fast Company*, March 12, 2014, www.fastcompany.com/3027135/inside-the-pixar-braintrust.

grow more and more like the One who gave her to you in the first place, which will in turn lead your marriage to heights of honesty, maturity, and intimacy it has never been to before.

Life-Changing Words

One final story on the power of listening and speaking the truth in love. I will never forget a moment just a few years ago when Ann spoke some hard, yet truthful words to me. She didn't pick the best time, but her words were indeed life-changing. The conversation happened sometime around 11:30 p.m. on a Sunday night. I had preached four times that day and had crawled into bed completely exhausted.

Ann and I quickly prayed together, and I was about ten seconds away from dreamland when I heard these words: "Sometimes I wish that the man who preaches to and leads our church would be the same man in our home." Since I was pretty much asleep, I wasn't sure I had heard her right, so I rolled over and said, "What did you just say?" She repeated her words . . . verbatim. This time I heard them loud and clear. I honestly couldn't believe we were going to go *there* at this hour, but it couldn't be stopped.

I asked for clarification. Ann said, "You are such a strong leader who stands on that stage week after week and leads us spiritually with power and grace. You pray with a fervency that is inspiring." This part made me feel pretty good, but I sensed a bomb was about to be dropped. Then she said, "But you are not that man at home. Here you often seem passive spiritually, and I sense that you don't want to lead me at all. I long for you to be the man here that you are at church."

Boom . . . direct hit.

I have to admit that Ann wrapped this truth in love, really

speaking it with grace and tenderness. But I also have to admit that I received it with no grace and no tenderness. I pretty much blew up, saying something like, "You don't know how good you have it. I'm the best husband I know, and I lead you better than any man on the planet!" Well, I might not have said the planet, but I definitely exaggerated just a bit. And then I added one more super mature comment: "I don't want to talk about this tonight. I'm exhausted from leading so strongly spiritually, and I'm going to sleep!" And that was that.

The next morning, I woke up to find that the hard truth spoken to me the night before was still there, staring me in the face. I went into my office, got on my knees, and asked God if what Ann had said was true. And you've probably already guessed what I heard. Yep, God confirmed every word. (I hate it when Ann is right!)

So now I had to actually deal with this truth spoken to me in love. Would I remain defensive and refuse to grow, or would I receive this truth as if it had come from God, and become the man and husband that my wife deserves and longs for?

It took some time, but I became thankful that Ann had the courage to speak a hard truth to me—because God used it to change me. It was time to step up. That's what men do: step up to become the men we are called by God to be through his power. I can't say I never again slipped back into laziness and passivity as a husband, but I can say that this truth changed me, and I am eternally grateful my wife had the courage to speak the truth.

That *was* love.

Nine

Tear Down That Wall

When our oldest son, CJ, was thirteen years old, he and I (Ann) got into a huge fight. He made me so mad that I exploded and then proceeded to ground him. But when my emotions began to settle, I felt remorse about the harshness of my response. As I drove him to school, I decided to apologize.

"CJ, I'm really sorry," I said. "I totally blew up on you, and it was uncalled for. I apologize. Let's try this again. Can you try to tell me what's going on inside your head right now?"

Angry and sullen, he just sat there with his arms folded across his chest. He looked at me, but said nothing. It was a move I was all too familiar with—yes, it reminded me of his father.

"Okay, don't do that," I said calmly. "Let's really talk about it."

But the silent treatment continued until we arrived at school. "Do not get out of the car until we have at least a bit of resolution," I said. He looked at me, opened the car door, got out, and walked into the school.

Now I was hot! I was so mad that I considered chasing him into the school, but I decided against it—although it might have made a more interesting story. Instead I drove away thinking to myself, *This is awful! I literally don't know what to do.*

I could have given up at that point—trust me, I wanted to. In fact, how many mothers and fathers have done just that in those extreme moments when it feels completely impossible for resolution to ever emerge from conflict with one's adolescent child? I felt this sense of hopelessness about the situation, but I knew I needed to do something else to reach out to him.

It's sad that sometimes the last thing we think about is praying. Sad, but true. Regardless, I finally came to my senses and prayed, "God, please help me! The first chapter of James says that 'if any of you lacks wisdom, you should ask God, who gives generously to all without finding fault,' so God, I *really* need your wisdom. I *really* need your help. I don't want this to go unresolved."

At that moment, I truly believe God gave me an idea. I went home and drew a picture—a crude sketch of a man facing a woman, and between them at their feet stood one lone brick. Then I put the picture on CJ's desk in his room. Later that afternoon after he came home from school, he migrated back downstairs with the picture in his hand. He looked puzzled.

"Mom, what is this? Is this your new attempt at art?"

"Oh good, you found it! *That* is a picture of what happened in our relationship this morning."

It was nothing but "crickets" on his end, so I just kept going, pointing to the page. "That woman is me, and the man is you. And that thing, or box, between us right there is supposed to be a brick—and that brick represents the fight we had this morning. It's between us because our fight is still unresolved."

"I'm not mad anymore about our fight this morning, Mom," he muttered.

"I'm not mad about it either, but the fact that our anger is gone doesn't mean that our fight is resolved or that the brick is gone. It's still there . . . it's just not resolved. And every single year, your dad and I see hundreds of marriages and relationships between parents and kids where there's a big fight, but they don't talk about it. They don't resolve it."

I could tell he was listening now.

"And do you know what happens to them?" He shrugged his shoulders. "CJ, they have one fight, and they form a brick. Then they have another fight, and they form another brick."

As I was talking, I picked up a pencil and started drawing one brick after another, stacking them. Now there was a high wall of many bricks standing between the two stick figures.

"After a while," I continued, "there are so many bricks of unresolved issues that a seemingly insurmountable wall has formed, and soon this couple can't hear each other, see each other, or even interact with each other. They are now isolated, hurt, and angry—and it's difficult for them to even have a good conversation, let alone a good relationship."

I paused to let the image really take shape in his mind. "I don't want that between us. Do you?"

"No, I don't," he said solemnly.

"So let's talk about how to get rid of the brick we formed today." He agreed, and I explained what was going on in my head when we were fighting, and also why I became angry and hurt. "What were *you* thinking?" I asked.

He told me his thoughts—as well as a teenage boy can. I apologized for yelling at him and hurting him. He apologized in return. Then we prayed together. Afterward, I took my pencil and erased all the bricks in the picture. "Let's never have any bricks—let alone a wall—in our relationship."

The Proactive Pursuit of Conflict Resolution

Maybe it's the fact that Dave's parents divorced when he was only seven. Maybe it's the fact that we've been speaking on the topic of marriage around the nation for so many years. Or maybe it's just become our hill to die on because our marriage almost died on it so many times. Regardless of the reason, conflict resolution is a high priority for Dave and me. We have learned the hard way that during a conflict, we must *both* pursue resolution. Instead of throwing verbal bricks at each other or using bricks of resentment to build a wall, we need to pick up the brick of conflict and resolve it.

But make no mistake, the priority is not just toward "resolution," but rather toward the "proactive pursuit" of resolution *at all costs.* Perhaps we've just met one too many people who, for whatever reason, failed to pursue or find this kind of resolution . . . and we've seen how this failure left their marriages and even their very selves broken. When resolution is no longer pursued by *both* parties, relationships are left to die. There is an urgency in our hearts toward this issue because we've witnessed far too many marriages perish as a result of a couple's neglecting to be *mutually* resolved to *ardently* seek resolution.

As I said before, early in our marriage, Dave would avoid conflict. Better said, he hated it! When an argument would erupt, as they always do in marriages, his solution was to just walk out of the room and leave me alone to deal with the aftermath. Our conflict would often remain unresolved for days and even months on end, which only led to more anger and frustration.

This anger eventually set up inside our hearts like concrete in the form of bitterness. Bitterness poisons marriage— especially when it's left to fester over the span of years. Perhaps you can relate, or perhaps not, but many couples feel isolated from each other simply because of some conflict they left unresolved decades ago.

Often, marital conflicts never find resolution because both

sides feel that the other is to blame. The last thing a marriage needs is *soul mates* arriving at a *stalemate*. You know the drill. Both of you wait for the other person to make the first move. It's like a staring contest for adults, but there are no winners.

Such a methodology for seeking resolution is no way to live, and it almost guarantees that a marriage will suffer. Instead, each spouse in a marriage should do their personal best to adopt this attitude toward moments or issues of conflict: "No matter who is most to blame here, I will take the initiative and move us toward resolution."

When two people take the initiative to move toward the same goal, this goal will be reached twice as easily and in half the time—even though it is super hard.

It's interesting to note the many varied and unique ways that the Scriptures lead us to be proactive when it comes to resolving conflict. We're told to "strive for peace with everyone" (Hebrews 12:14 ESV), to "be quick to listen" (James 1:19), and to always be "speaking the truth in love" (Ephesians 4:15). *Strive. Be quick. Speak.* These are imperatives that lead us to action, not passive concepts to be admired from afar.

Matthew takes it even further: "So if you are offering your gift at the altar and there remember that your brother has something against you, leave your gift there before the altar and go. First be reconciled to your brother, and then come and offer your gift" (Matthew 5:23–24 ESV). Rarely do you hear this one preached in a church, because most pastors would rather that you *stay* and give your money than *go* and work on the conflict. Ha!

But not so with Jesus. He values reconciliation in relationships as one of the highest priorities in life. No matter what it takes, go now and make this thing right. Don't wait for your spouse to act; you move . . . now!

What an incredible, but so often overlooked, glimpse into the way God feels about unresolved conflict in our lives! Yes, there are moments to cool off, but those must never become the ending points of the conversation. Cooling off should be for the purpose of preparing oneself to better approach the other person in the process of seeking resolution together. Every marriage has moments where one spouse offends the other. The *offense* is an act, but to stay *offended* is a choice. We must choose to move toward a resolution to this offense.

Contrary to popular belief, ignoring conflict doesn't make it go away; it makes it worse. Ignoring conflict is akin to turning up your car radio so you won't hear that annoying grinding noise coming from your engine. Give it a few miles, and the noise will be the least of your problems.

Here is an immutable truth concerning relationships: *When it comes to conflict, nothing is worse than doing nothing.*

It's just as the old adage says, "If you aim at nothing, you'll hit it every time." But when you push through into the conflict for the purpose of collectively working through it, you will come out stronger and better—and even more in love than you were before. Intimacy and trust do not just appear on the mountaintops of our easiest moments. They are also forged in the dark unknown of those valleys that we choose to pass through together, even when it would be easier to avoid them.

Good Marriages Sometimes Sleep On It

You may be wondering, *Doesn't the Bible say we shouldn't let the sun go down on our anger?*—a reference to Paul's words in his letter to the Ephesians: "'In your anger do not sin': Do not let the sun go down while you are still angry, and do not give the devil a foothold" (4:26–27).

But this passage is often misunderstood. When we were first married, we thought it was a clear instruction not to go to bed if we had an unresolved conflict. On some occasions, we'd stay up until two or three in the morning. I can remember yelling at Dave as he nodded off, "How can you fall asleep? You don't care about our relationship!"

My exhausted husband would reply, "I really do, but I'm so sleepy."

"But we've got to do this. The Bible says we've got to resolve this before we go to sleep!"

As you can imagine, those early-morning arguments rarely ended well. But as we have looked more closely at this passage, we've come to realize that it shouldn't be taken quite so literally. The apostle Paul is speaking here of the need to resolve conflict quickly, but he's not setting an artificial deadline. I even remember Dave once saying to me at the very beginning of an argument that had just started between us right before bedtime, "This 'resolve it before the sun goes down' deal can't be literal—the sun went down hours ago, and we just started fighting. We're good! We have until tomorrow night to resolve this thing!"

No, the principle here is that we should not let our conflicts linger for days and weeks. We should resolve them quickly.

Sometimes it actually helps to take a break before talking again, just to take some time to process what's going on. Sleep on it—sometimes your whole perspective will change. A little space and rest can help you realize what led to the conflict in the first place, as well as your role in it. You may realize that what seemed to be a major problem yesterday looks much smaller by the light of the morning sun.

In fact, there have been times when I would ask Dave in the middle of a fight what he was feeling at that exact moment.

It would drive me crazy when he would respond with something like, "I honestly don't know." I thought he was just trying to avoid conflict yet again. But the next morning, he would come to me and say, "Hey, I've had some time to think, and now I know what I'm feeling about our conflict last night." I've learned over the years that Dave just needs some time to process. He was keeping quiet the night before because he didn't want to lash out in anger when he didn't even fully know why he was mad in the first place. Sleeping on it was actually the best thing for us to do so we could reach a resolution.

But remember that if you do take a break, you need to be sure to set a time to talk about it the next day. Don't let it ride, and don't let it slide.

Use Soft Words to Keep a Conflict from Escalating

Take a moment and think about the worst arguments you've had over the years—with your spouse, your parents, or your friends. If you are a parent yourself, think of the arguments you've witnessed between your children. Isn't it all too easy for an argument to escalate? Accusations are traded, temperatures rise, and voices go from loud to deafening.

Things can get out of control before you know what hit you—and after that, it's hard to stop a train that's careening down the tracks.

But God has not left us alone to the proverbial train wrecks that our marriages and families become when angry moments go unchecked: "A soft answer turns away wrath, but a harsh word stirs up anger" (Proverbs 15:1 ESV). These are some of the most recognizable words you will find in Scripture, perhaps so recognizable that we subconsciously dismiss them as simplistic rhetoric. *Uh, of course speaking softly will help us avoid arguments. The problem is, when I'm that upset, I don't want to speak softly!*

But the truth of this passage is so much deeper than we often give it credit for. Harsh words do indeed stir up anger, so to avoid the inevitable downward spiral, someone has to practically say, "I'm going to tread gently here. I'm not going to raise my voice. I'm going to be calm, not angry."

It may *feel* impossible to control your emotions in an argument, but that doesn't make it true. It *is* possible, and the quicker we believe rightly that it is, as God's Word has shown us, the quicker we make room for growth in this area. This is one of those moments in which you can ask God to do in your situation what you could never do on your own. With God's help you can control your tongue.

A few years ago, one of the headlights went out in my car. At the time it malfunctioned, I had just been asked to speak at a conference about a month later, so I asked Dave if he would replace the headlight before my five-hour road trip.

"Absolutely," he said. "I'll get that done before your trip."

One week passed. Then two. Each week, I asked Dave again, "Did you fix the headlight yet?"

"No, but I will," he replied each time. This carried on all the way up to the day before I was slated to leave for the conference. A little flustered, I asked him about it again, and he said, "I have a meeting in the morning, but on the way home, I'll fix the headlight, and then you'll be good to go. I'm not going to forget."

On the day of my trip, he pulled into the driveway a little late. I had already placed my suitcase in the back of the car. Happy to see him before I left, I gave him a kiss and prepared to embark on my journey. Just before leaving, something inside cued me to simply double-check, so I asked, "You fixed the headlight, right?"

In slow motion, an expression of absolute panic broke out across his face. You can imagine how angry I was.

"You've had a *month* to fix that headlight!"

He was scrambling now, trying to figure out a way to repair more than the headlight. "Okay, I'm going to do it right now! I'll follow you to Kmart," he huffed in frustration.

"No!" I yelled. "It's too late!"

I slammed the door shut, but as I sped off in our Honda, I could hear Dave yelling at the boys to get into the van. The last thing I saw was Dave shoving CJ, Austin, and Cody into the van; shutting the door; and forgetting to even put Cody into his car seat. I hoped to myself that one of the older kids would buckle him in.

"He's a negligent husband *and* dad!" I angrily fumed as I sped down the road.

I was driving at the time, white-knuckling the steering wheel in sheer rage. In my mind, I began to list all the reasons that I was such a good wife and that Dave obviously didn't love me in return.

I left him and the boys a refrigerator full of meals they could eat while I was gone. I stuffed that negative thought deep inside.

I even put Scripture notes around the house to encourage him.

Another ugly thought I wadded up and tucked even deeper down.

What did he do for me? Nothing! I'm such a good wife, but does he ever even think of me? I'm his last priority. He doesn't care.

I took all of these thoughts—and more—and buried them in my heart to germinate and grow . . . and to possibly use as ammunition later. I was right, and he was wrong. It felt good to be right, and I wanted to sit awhile in my self-righteousness and let my anger fester.

The only thing worse than *highway hypnosis* is *hypothetical hypnosis*—and I was experiencing both. I was letting him have it in my mind, and even in the recesses of my thoughts, things were getting out of control. It was one of those moments when I knew God was trying to get a word in amid all the ranting my brain was doing, but I really didn't want to listen. So I turned on the radio—really loud!

I could sense God saying, "Take it out and give it to me."

No! I didn't want to do it! So I told God, "I feel like Dave doesn't see me. He doesn't care about me. He doesn't love me. I'm not a priority to him!" But as I was trying to resist God's invitation to give it to him, I ended up venting all my feelings before him.

We pulled into Kmart, and Dave sprinted into the store to buy a new headlight lamp.

As I sat there waiting for him, I realized I had a choice. I could hold on to this offense—this hurt—and use it as ammunition later when Dave and I would painfully hash out this whole ridiculous scenario after I returned from the conference. Or I could give it to God and ask him for the strength and empowerment to speak gently. It was a hard decision, but I knew that if I chose anger, the end result would be painful, even if I was right—which I was.

This way of winning suddenly didn't sound very much like a win to me. So instead, I prayed a short, exasperated prayer: "Lord, I'm giving it to you. You know my heart, and I know that you love me, so I surrender it to you. I surrender Dave to you again. Help me to be the wife I need to be because right now, I just want to hurt him."

By this point, Dave had come back outside and had finished replacing the headlight. He walked over to my car window and said, "I'm so sorry. Are you okay?" I could tell he was waiting to get blasted, and rightfully so.

But it seemed that God had honored my frustrated prayer because, to my surprise, I just replied, "Honey, I'm okay." And with those three soft words, a conflict that could have risen to epic proportions was instead defused.

Yes, we eventually talked it out after I returned from the conference because there were obviously communication and follow-through issues that we needed to address and agree on, but the situation didn't hang over us for the weekend like a toxic cloud.

Sometimes, using soft words can keep a broken levee from flooding your marriage. Proverbs says it best: "Starting a quarrel is like breaching a dam; so drop the matter before a dispute breaks out" (17:14).

Power of the Tongue

Whether you realize it or not, your words are incredibly powerful: "The tongue has the power of life and death" (Proverbs 18:21). The Bible also tells us, "Do not let any unwholesome talk come out of your mouths, but only what is helpful for building others up according to their needs, that it may benefit those who listen" (Ephesians 4:29).

Words are the bricks of your marriage—for better or for worse. You can throw that brick through a window and possibly put someone in the hospital, or you can wisely use it to build a safe haven where joy and safety surround your marriage on all sides. With your words, you have the power to tear your spouse apart or to give him life, encouragement, and grace.

Remember the story from the first year of our marriage when I told Dave that "marrying you was the biggest mistake of my life"? The reality is that the actual biggest mistake of my life was *saying* those words to Dave. Can you imagine how devastating it must have been for him to hear those words from his young wife?

This particular brick was dangerous, and Dave has thrown his fair share through my windows as well. So after that experience, Dave and I set a rule: we vowed to never threaten each other with divorce. Divorce would not be part of our vocabulary.

We've honored that rule over the years, but I must admit it has been more difficult to do so in heated moments. That's the point though—we had made the decision before the sparks started flying so that we wouldn't burn our house down with our words of anger.

Another way to help yourself speak gently when you're in the middle of a big conflict is to choose to *believe the best about each other rather than assume the worst.* Just as extreme grief or insecurity can cloud our spiritual beliefs, anger clouds our belief in the person we're angry at. They stop looking like the beloved bride or groom of our youth and start looking more like the little green one-eyed monster Mike Wazowski from *Monsters, Inc.*—minus Billy Crystal's charm and wit.

Remind yourself *now* to tell yourself *then* that the beautiful, two-eyed person you married is still in there somewhere, even though the good traits may be eclipsed by the anger and conflict you are experiencing at the moment. If you stop believing in who they are, you will stop treating them like who they are.

You may have to dig deep to bring back to the light of day that part of your spouse you once thought worthy of your celebration and affection. The apostle Paul leads us to do just that: "Finally, brothers and sisters, whatever is true, whatever is noble, whatever is right, whatever is pure, whatever is lovely, whatever is admirable—if anything is excellent or praiseworthy—think about such things" (Philippians 4:8).

I encourage you to reread this verse a couple of times. Then take out a pen and paper and write down the things that are true, noble, lovely, and admirable about your spouse. Again, make this a list of the things you've always believed about him or her, not just the recent discoveries you've made in moments of adversity that have tainted your viewpoint and left you disillusioned.

Chances are you'll come up with a pretty impressive list. Then read through those things that are true of your spouse, letting your mind dwell on them. This simple exercise can soften your attitude and perhaps even provide some insight into your present conflict.

And in general, thinking differently will lead to more gentle answers that turn away wrath.

Forgive Each Other

Paul doesn't pull any punches when it comes to the practical actions we should take in directly facing conflict: "Get rid of all bitterness, rage and anger, brawling and slander, along with every form of malice. Be kind and compassionate to one another, forgiving each other, just as in Christ God forgave you" (Ephesians 4:31–32).

There are two equal and opposite sides to this equation. Obviously, one critical element of being proactive in resolving conflict is asking forgiveness from those you have wronged. This is key—and those who are not willing to see their own wrong and request forgiveness for it will always be crippled by conflict.

But the flip side of the coin is also true. If you have been hurt, you must also do the forgiving—"just as in Christ God forgave you." This is a command, not a suggestion. If you've been forgiven by Christ, you are commanded to forgive others.

Paul's words certainly do not speak to getting revenge, even though this is the normal human reaction when we've been wronged. We want payback! We go to movies and cheer when the good guy wreaks vengeance on the evil ones who hurt him. But this is no movie, and we are not "good guys" in the sense that we do good things. We are the "good guys" who have been transformed in our hearts and declared to be such because Jesus has done all the work for us—and his main work is forgiveness of those whose decisions ultimately killed him. We are those whose sin killed him. We are those whom he has forgiven. We are the *good guys* only because he is the *Good God*, and our first order of goodness is a reflection of his first order of goodness—it is the act of forgiveness.

Forgiveness means releasing the offender from the obligation to repay a debt. Often we don't want to release the offender; we enjoy being in what I call "the grip of the grudge." We hold grudges for years, allowing bitterness to continually harden our hearts. Then one day, we realize that this isn't living. This kind of life isn't making us happy, but we don't know what to do because the layers of hardness are years deep. Just recall the story of Dave and his dad in chapter 7. It was only after Dave forgave his dad that he was set free from his decades-long, deep-seated anger.

Surrender to God

This is the last of our principles on resolving conflict, but it really should come first. The problem is that we often can't hear this particular principle because we will skip over it, chalking it up to something uber-spiritual that only pastors and super-Christians apply to real life.

But now that we've drilled down into the origins of conflict and our own roles in it, perhaps our hearts can hear this. Besides, if you try to apply everything we've mentioned so far but fail to grasp this point, you'll lose it all anyway. This is the linchpin: only by going vertical and surrendering your life daily to Christ will you find the ability to resolve conflict with your spouse.

Surrender is not an act of religiosity but an act of being completely honest with God. If anger and bitter words are all you have to bring to the trading table, can you be honest and courageous enough to talk to God in the way you are truly feeling, not in the way you think he wants you to feel? News flash: he's not going to blush at your anger-laced words; he's already hearing it in your heart anyway. Can you abandon your personal will to win so that your marriage can win instead? Can you bring your worst and trust that God promises to trade it for his best?

Surrender is honesty with God that leads to the abandonment of one's own plans and rights because of the belief that what God has for us can be trusted to be so much better than what we have for ourselves—even if we have to lose (or surrender) to experience it.

You may feel totally unable to use soft words in a conflict, to truly listen, to speak the truth in love, to move toward resolution, to forgive—or to do these things day after day, week after week, and year after year. What a daunting and intimidating task—to live out the vows you made on your wedding day. They are impossible.

But *God can give us the power to do what feels impossible.*

In fact, surrender is really all about power. When we give up trying to do this in our own strength, God meets us right there and supplies a power far beyond anything we could ever muster on our own. Remember, he is the one who raises dead things, not you. He can give each of us a power that's not natural; it's supernatural.

The need to surrender is a common thread interwoven throughout the stories we've told in this book so far. So many times, I have been involved in conflicts where I find myself unable to move forward unless I am willing to surrender—and that usually looks like praying and giving everything to God. Nothing positive or transformative happens until I come to the point where I invite him into the conflict and say, "God, I want you to be a part of this relationship, a part of this conflict, and I want you to take control of my life. I can't reach resolution on my own. I can't get rid of my anger. I can't get rid of my resentment and my bitterness."

I hear him answer through the whisper of his Scriptures, the whisper of his people, or sometimes the whisper in my heart, but every time I surrender, God is gracious to remind me, "I know you can't. But I can." And what happens next is amazing; it's like a door swings open to the working of the Holy Spirit in my once bitter and angry heart.

The center of a conflict is an ugly state to be in. While we are in it, we so often become focused on what the *other* person is doing wrong, as if we instinctively believe the conflict will somehow go away if the *other* person repents and changes. But *your* surrender to God requires *your* humility, not that of your spouse. The only humility you can do anything about is your own, so the question is: Will you be humble before him first so you can also be humble before others?

If you will, trust me, it will be a sweet surrender.

The Fruit of Our Labor

Conflict resolution is a skill we must practice over and over again, much like perfecting a golf swing. Perfection may not be possible, but progress is. Remember the story of my fight with thirteen-year-old CJ? Fast-forward ten years.

One night, I walked into the living room and turned on the lights, only to find CJ (now twenty-three years old) sitting in the dark on the couch. Beside him, but on the opposite end, was his beautiful fiancée, Robin. I apologized for interrupting them and left the room.

The next morning, I asked CJ why they were sitting in the dark not talking. He nonchalantly said, "Oh, we were in a fight and working it out."

Confused, I blurted out, "But I didn't hear you talking or yelling?"

He didn't seem surprised by my comment. He simply said they had taken turns communicating what each of them were feeling and were upset about. However, before the other person would respond, they would first take time to think about what they wanted to communicate and how they should say it best to be better understood and received.

I honestly don't remember if I even said anything to CJ. Instead, I ran upstairs to find Dave. "Honey," I yelled, "a miracle has happened. Our children are way better at resolving conflict than we are!"

The fruit of our marital labors—to keep reaching out, to talk, to listen, to forgive, and especially to pray—had never tasted so sweet.

Ten

"ALL I HEAR IS,

'Boo!' "

One day, I (Ann) was stressing out, racking my brain trying to figure out how to find the time to work on my talk for the Mothers of Preschoolers (MOPS) event only two days away. With three little boys careening through our house, aimlessly throwing any and every object they could find, what should have been a simple and enjoyable task instead felt impossible.

The molehill had become nothing less than mountainous.

Then it hit me—a thought, that is. (I had also been hit by several of the boys' miscellaneous projectiles.) This was a recurring thought: *Things would be so much easier if Dave wasn't so busy and could help out more. Seriously, why does he have three jobs anyway?* Dave always said it was to help us financially, but sometimes it honestly felt like he was just using his many commitments as excuses to get out of the house—and out of the craziness we were living under in those days.

I was stuck, and I needed a little help from him—and that's when suddenly I had an idea. Ask Dave! So I called him and said, "Hey, hon, how would you feel about speaking with me on Tuesday to the women at MOPS? They would *love* to hear my husband speak alongside me about marriage. I bet a man's perspective is just what they need!"

"Sure! If my calendar is open, I'd be happy to do it with you."

The stress immediately evaporated, and I took a big sigh of relief. Even though I had been upset with him, it's always *way* easier—and honestly, way more fun—to speak alongside Dave than to do so alone. So that was that.

Until it wasn't.

Tuesday morning arrived, and even as we were getting ready and shuffling the boys off to school, I felt that old familiar tug of disappointment. It was the same old whisper. *Why do I do everything around here? Dave hardly helps at all. He doesn't even know the routine or what needs to be done!* This internal monologue of griping had become my secret habitual pattern—so much so that the complaining in my head had become as familiar as brushing my teeth or putting on my clothes. By that point, I was doing it without even thinking about it.

And yet, here we were, on our way to share together on the topic of having a healthy marriage. *Yikes! What was I going to say?* The truth was, I believed I was doing *everything* in this marriage! If Dave would only help more or even just listen a little more, I knew we would be great. As you can imagine, these were *not* the thoughts I wanted to share with the women. How encouraging would that be?

We arrived at the venue, and women began filling the room. I could tell by their energy that they were excited about hearing our insights on marriage. They probably felt like we were experts since we had written and delivered many series on the subject at church, not to mention that we had spoken at many weekend marriage conferences around the country.

They had no idea what was really going on—honestly, neither did I.

We opened with a few introductory remarks, and then Dave just started going! He spoke with enthusiasm and vigor. He began to share things I had never heard him say before. For some reason, he seemed more excited than usual to express his thoughts, because the words couldn't seem to leave his mouth quickly enough.

The talk began as we sat beside each other on stools, but it didn't take long for him to stand up and start moving around to more passionately convey his ideas. The room was mesmerized—honestly, so was I. Despite all of our issues, I had really locked in to what he was expressing to these young moms.

Dave was laser-focused. "Women, I don't know if you realize this, but somewhere along the line, most of your husbands were cheered and applauded for the things they did. Most often, little boys have moms or dads cheering for them, 'Good job!'" He paused for a moment and then continued. "And as we get older and begin to discover the things we're good at doing, there is usually someone there again—like a teacher or coach—cheering and applauding us with, 'Good job!'"

As Dave was saying all this, he began clapping his hands very hard each time he said the words "good job." He continued. "I played quarterback in college, so every weekend there were people in the stadium cheering for the team and cheering for me! 'Good job. You're the man!' they would say." Again, Dave clapped his hands together enthusiastically after each "good job."

"When I met Ann, she basically said, 'Of all the men in the world, I choose *you*, Dave Wilson! You're the man!'" Again, another rousing clap from Dave.

I was still seated on my little stool and thinking, *Man, this stuff is good! I've never heard him say anything like this before.*

But my marveling was a bit premature.

Suddenly, his tone changed and the enthusiasm bottomed out of his voice. He slowly and distinctly uttered words I will never forget.

"Then we get married." He paused as if he had just broken bad news. "After a long day, we walk in the door, and all we hear is, 'Boo! Boo! Boo!'"

The women in the room began to chuckle sheepishly. I was dumbstruck. Dave, on the other hand, was apparently just plain dumb because, without missing a beat in his motivational discourse, he turned toward me and began shouting in my direction his last "boo" with his hands cupped around his mouth like a megaphone. As he did, our eyes met. In that moment, I could tell from the look on his face that for the first time in this whole out-of-the-body experience, his brain was actually thinking thoughts. I could almost overhear his inner monologue: *Oh crap, I probably should have passed this by Ann first.*

Ya think?

Besides my extreme embarrassment in the moment, I was genuinely wondering what in the world he was talking about. In all the years we had been married, he had never ever expressed anything like this. Needless to say, fifteen years is a very long time to let something of this magnitude go unsaid.

I kid you not when I say that I seriously do not remember how we finished that talk with those young women. I went blank . . . and possibly cross-eyed. I do, however, remember with meticulous detail our ride home together.

"What in the world happened back there? Is that really how you feel? Do you really think I boo you all the time?"

Dave looked as shocked as I felt. "Honestly," he explained, "I have *no idea* where that came from. It just started coming out, and as I kept talking, I realized that this is exactly what I've been feeling."

Feeling both wounded and offended, I quickly jabbed back. "I am *helping* you! I'm the one who really knows you and sees all the good and bad. I'm helping you to be better!"

He didn't raise his voice. "It doesn't feel like help," he quietly responded. "It feels like a constant 'boo.' I feel like I can't do anything right. You critique everything I do, and you remind me of all the things I'm not doing and should be doing—heck, and what other husbands are doing." He paused to weigh whether he wanted to speak what was up next in his mental queue. "Really, who wants to come home to that?"

Silence filled the car and hovered over us like fog the rest of the drive home. My head was swarming with thoughts. *Is Dave right? Have I been booing him constantly?* I battled back and forth between feeling bad and feeling justified about the situation.

He needs me to speak truth to him, I reasoned internally. *I am helping him to get better. In fact, I am helping the Holy Spirit, since Dave's probably too busy to hear the voice of God!*

Yeah, that last one didn't quite sit right within me—I could tell the Spirit was convicting me even as the thought materialized. *Ugh!* But thankfully, we pulled into our driveway and the whole awkward event was finally over and done—or at least I thought it was.

"Cheer for Him"

As it turned out, the issue was not resolved. The thick fog never lifted. For the next several days, I just couldn't get this question out of my mind: *Do I really boo Dave?*

The punching and counterpunching going on within my internal reasoning was far from any peaceful resolution. In fact, it was only entering round two—and I had no idea how many rounds were in this fight.

But somewhere in the mental melee, I began to actually ponder Dave's accusation. I wondered what things would be like if I were to constantly cheer for him—you know, tell him he was awesome all the time and such. The answer was swift and clear: it wouldn't work. Just think about it. If I did that, then Dave would think I was happy with the way he was treating me, specifically in the areas of helping around the house and his role as a father.

But as I thought through the way I was thinking this through (yes, you heard me correctly), I noticed something else for the first time. I sounded more like a boss—with Dave as my direct report and my corporate task being to evaluate his job performance—than his wife. I was finally beginning to see Dave's point.

But again, I rationalized that if I didn't critique Dave's performance, he would think I was satisfied, and thus I would be enabling him to remain where he was instead of growing him into the husband and father he needed to be. And that wouldn't be good, right?

I went on like this for several days until I felt God tugging at my heart. As much as I didn't want to admit it, I knew he was calling me to surrender this situation—to give him my worries, fears, and disappointments. I could tell that God wanted me to ask *him* what he wanted me to do. Perhaps you can empathize with my hesitation to give in—I had that familiar feeling of not wanting to ask God because I was afraid of what he might ask of me. The truth was, I didn't want to become a doormat. Or lose my voice. Or feel like I was a passive, weak-willed woman—the kind who can easily be taken advantage of.

But finally, having exhausted my own efforts, I took a dive and let God win. I sat before him and complained. I told him everything I was feeling. I shared all my fears, and I asked him what he wanted me to do.

It didn't take very long to sense a still, small voice some-where deep in my soul: "Cheer for him."

I'm not necessarily proud of my first reaction, but neverthe-less, it went something like, *Blah blah blah—surely that isn't God!* Even as first responders prove their bravery by instinctively rushing into danger, my initial reaction was proving something as well . . . but what was it? What was this deeper issue I was facing of not wanting to praise and cheer Dave on? Why had I become so controlling?

Once again, I felt the Holy Spirit nudging me to observe my thoughts, as well as the words that were coming out of my mouth—and more specifically, the words I *was not* planning to speak or the words I wasn't meticulously measuring for maxi-mum impact. So for the next week, I kept track of what I was thinking about Dave—and I mean what I was *really* thinking about him. Let me tell you, those thoughts were not pretty at all.

Even in my head I was continually nagging him.

I was constantly comparing my hard life with his easy cake-walk of a life—always dwelling on all the ways *I* had given up so much and was doing so much, while *he* had given up nothing and was doing relatively nothing. All around, I basically felt that his life was a breeze.

As I tuned in more intently to the radio station of my own mind, I even discovered that Dave was actually right about at least one thing: I had definitely been comparing him to other husbands who seemed more romantic or more attuned to their wives' needs. How devastating that must have been to him. To be quite honest, I was shocked by the negativity of my own thought patterns. It had become such a habit to think this way that "What's Negative about Dave" had become my new norm—the call sign of my mental radio station. *You're listening to WNAD. All bad thoughts about Dave . . . all the time.*

Since part one began with the evaluation of my thought life, it was time for part two: keeping track of the things that actually came out of my mouth. After some careful examination, I discovered that my words were not necessarily mean—not necessarily. I would call them something more like sophisticated nagging.

Potato, potahto.

"Why can't we have a family devotional like other families do?"

Boo!

"You're not going to be home again to put the boys to bed and pray for them?"

Boo!

"You didn't change the oil or fix the car or mow the lawn or take out the garbage . . . again? Fine! I'll do it . . . again!"

Double boo!

This was our constant dialogue about practically everything. But the worst part was that it became apparent that I very rarely praised Dave or thanked him for anything. I wasn't a monster; I just thought, *That's his job, so why would I thank him? I do everything with no thanks from anyone.*

Wow . . . I hadn't even noticed that I had developed quite the martyr complex. I was a mess! I was ashamed of myself. I knew this stuff and taught this stuff, and yet I hadn't even realized what I had slipped into. The Bible says, "The thief comes only to steal and kill and destroy; I [Jesus] have come that they may have life, and have it to the full" (John 10:10). Somehow—subtly and slowly—I had allowed Satan to slip into my marriage, and he was trying to steal, kill, and destroy our family.

But even though there was an enemy present, I needed to own up to my part in the whole process. And I needed to let

God take care of Dave. My job was to *respect* Dave! I knew and taught as much from the fifth chapter of Ephesians, where Paul calls wives to respect their husbands. I just hadn't realized that I wasn't applying this truth in our home. *At all.*

It was time to change—so I prayed. "Father God, forgive me! I have not been respecting Dave, and, in fact, I have been nagging him and criticizing him, and I haven't been cheering for him. I give you my marriage, and I give you my life. I ask that you help me to see Dave the way you see him. I give up my control of trying to change him. And I ask that you would give me power through your Holy Spirit to cheer and appreciate Dave, even when I don't want to—even when I feel like he doesn't deserve it. I'm asking that Dave would know how much you love him by the way I treat him. I can only do this with your help, Father! Amen."

It started with that simple prayer, but it didn't end there.

A Process of Transformation

I continued to address these issues by spending time with God each day, asking for his help and asking him to change *me*! It started slowly, and I certainly didn't change overnight, but in small ways at first, God began a process of transformation in me. It started with me simply thanking Dave for the things he was doing—coaching the boys' teams, emptying the dishwasher (even if I had to ask), cleaning up, mowing the lawn, et cetera— and yes, to my shock and awe, there were enough things that Dave was doing to warrant an "et cetera." Who knew?

One evening a few months later, I set the food on the table as we prepared to pray. All three boys were ravenous, but I still made them wait a few moments. I had to tell them something very important. "Hey, before we pray and eat, I want to stop for a minute and say thanks to Dad for working so hard every single day to provide this meal—and every meal for our home. We should thank him for working so hard to provide all that we have." Then I turned to Dave and continued. "It's easy to take your hard work for granted. Thanks, honey!"

Dave's face was beaming as we shared the moment. The boys? Not so much. They just asked if they could eat already, not recognizing or caring about this momentous display of respect. Later that night, Dave told me my words were the best thing that had happened to him all week. *What?* A few measly words that took less than a minute to convey? Seriously?

Yep . . . all he heard in that moment was applause.

As I began to be more consistent in cheering Dave instead of booing him, I could tell he was a little incredulous, as if to say, *What are you up to?* But what at first might have seemed forced or insincere soon became a habit. I was now honestly looking for the positive things that Dave was doing—things in which I could genuinely encourage him.

Over time, I realized that my nagging had not been aimed only at Dave; I was continually nagging our three sons as well. Maybe I thought critique was a good teaching strategy . . . who knows? Regardless, I set out with the same mission toward them: to observe their positive actions and character qualities, and to praise them and thank them more than I ever had before.

These were not just external disciplines; I began to see God change me inwardly. My crusty, dissatisfied heart was starting to soften. Joy began to displace my discontentment. Peace began to weave its way in me as my anger and bitterness began to ebb. I found a new thankfulness in my position of influence as a woman, and our home changed—because God was changing *me*! Encouragement and gratitude were now becoming common threads in our family.

"All I Hear Is, 'Boo!'"

And no, I did not lose my voice. Rather, I took my complaints to God first and asked him to help me speak my heart and mind in a way that Dave could really hear—in a way that didn't overwhelm him with constant booing. It's certainly not that I stopped teaching and training our children. The change was simple: positive words of affirmation flowed in abundance so that when negative words needed to be shared, they could actually be heard—and swallowed—a little easier.

Women, we have so much power! Our words have the power to bring life and death. I want to be a woman that my family can't wait to come home to. Outside our homes, our husbands, children, and friends are being bombarded with negativity. We can be the ones to bolster their sails and bring them joy. As Dave says, "A man will always go where he's cheered!"

I want my man to come home.

My Biggest Cheerleader

I (Dave) would love to add my perspective about the way Ann's "booing" of me over the years has been completely transformed. When I first told her several decades ago that I felt booed at home, I meant it. I was feeling respected in many different areas of my life, but not at home by Ann.

My feelings were hard for her to hear at first, so much so that we fought about it for quite some time. But all I can say is that now she is my biggest cheerleader. I honestly now feel respected and cheered on by her every day. And when I come home and she is wearing that cheerleader outfit (the one with the big "D" on it), man oh man, does that feel good!

In all seriousness, I would love to tell wives that when you speak words of life and respect to us as men, it changes us for the better. Years ago, Ann's attitude and words toward me totally changed. She used to nag me and critique almost everything I did—and there were valid reasons for doing so. But the bottom line was that I could never really satisfy her. I felt that I was constantly letting her down.

I knew she *loved* me, but I also felt that she didn't really *like* me. But a few months after that "boo" moment, she began to treat me differently. She began to encourage me and thank me for who I was and what I was doing for her and the kids. She began to speak words of life over me that changed me.

Specifically, she would say, "You know, you really are a good man and a great husband." I would say to myself, *No, I'm not*. But her consistent encouragement made me want to become the man she said I was, even though I wasn't there yet. I was definitely *not yet* the man she said I was, but because she said I was, I rose up to become more like the man she said I already was . . . I'm sure that all made perfect sense!

A wife's words have power over her husband. Negative attitudes and words of "boo" do not motivate men, even if we deserve them. I'm not saying we can never hear criticism or correction, because that is just a part of healthy communication in a marriage. I'm talking more about the general conversational tone permeating the relationship.

Men are motivated and empowered to change by cheering and by respect of their personal value as a man in this marriage apart from their duties. This value is something most men question and feel insecure about. Respecting someone doesn't mean you are ignoring their obvious faults or dismissing their need to improve; it means you are acknowledging their value and potential, even when they're struggling to reflect or live up to them.

I know it doesn't always make sense, but just try it and see what happens. I promise you, booing and merciless critiquing just don't work. Why not try God's way of respect and see where it leads? You may have a new husband in a year—or maybe even a month! And especially if you put on that cheerleader outfit . . .

Sorry, I couldn't resist.

Eleven

WHAT EVERY WIFE

Longs For

There I (Dave) was, standing outside our church building between services on a Sunday morning. The day was off to a great start, as we had already had incredible services in two jam-packed auditoriums. When you are a pastor, Sundays like these leave you feeling revved up. And the best news was that it wasn't over yet; there was still one service to go. In fact, I was feeling so good that I was high-fiving people as they walked in for the final service of the day. Plus I was already greatly anticipating—as all pastors do on late Sunday mornings—what would happen at home directly after this service . . .

I would soon be taking a nap.

But my visions of sleepy bliss proved to be premature.

Just before I headed back into the auditorium for the final service, I looked out in the parking lot to see my lovely Ann arriving at the church in her car. Well, it was more like she was taking the checkered flag at the Indy 500. I kid you not when I say that Ann was laying down some serious rubber in our lot. I was a bit alarmed.

But my internal alarm began screaming even louder when I

realized where she was headed: an empty parking spot right by the front door of the church. Such a find was rare and valuable at our church—the pot of gold at the end of the fire lane. Like a stunt driver in *The Fast and the Furious*, she whipped the car to a perfectly timed stop right in this primo parking spot. Vin Diesel would have been proud.

Moments later, Ann emerged from the car with our two sons, Austin and Cody. As she walked toward the front door, she saw me and broke into a four-lane smile, obviously feeling very good about her parking spot. After all, it was the best spot in the whole lot.

"Hi, honey!" she said with a grin. "Look at the spot God gave me today!"

I scowled and grunted, "Move the car now."

She paused, taken aback by my curt command. Then she quickly retorted, "I'm not moving the car. God gave me that spot."

"God did not give you that spot. Move the car now or I'll move it."

It was obvious that I was *not* a happy camper. Keep in mind that as we are having this less-than-pleasant discussion, I was also welcoming people to our church with the fakest smile that has ever been faked. I was getting more heated by the moment. Finally I turned to Austin and said, "Austin, take the keys and move the car *now*!"

At that point, Ann jumped in front of Austin and said, "He is not moving the car!"

I could feel my blood boiling. This time my words made the quick trip from speaking to yelling, even though they were still uttered under my breath since people were walking right beside us into the church. "I've got to go preach. You move that car, and you move it *now*!"

At this point, you are probably wondering what the big deal was. Why was I so fired up about something as trivial as a parking spot? It will help if I explain my side of this story.

As one of the founding pastors of Kensington (that's our church name), I was honored to be a part of the core team that developed our core values. These were the values we built the church on—values we hold very near and dear to our identity.

One of those core values was that the unchurched person matters greatly. The outsider who has never been to Kensington is the very person we've designed our weekend experiences for. We want them to feel valued and appreciated. So we decided early on that a great way to demonstrate their value to us was to save the best parking spots for them. That meant that the spots right by the front doors were—and have always been—theirs.

How seriously do we take this parking pledge? Let's put it this way: we have all new members raise their right hands when joining our church and state that they will now take the worst parking spots in the lot and leave the closest spots for those who are new to Kensington. Of course, this is all done in fun, but the principle behind the pledge of preferring the first-time guest is something we take very seriously. In fact, all of our pastors—including myself—park in the very back of the lot. It's a quarter-mile walk, sometimes in frigid Michigan weather.

This is no "afterthought" core value—it defines who we are in a big way.

Now do you see why I was so hot? I just couldn't believe that Ann was violating a core foundational principle of our church. Everyone there knew how important this value was, and here was the pastor's wife zooming into the parking lot like Danica Patrick (or "Ann"ica Patrick, if you will), breaking the rules. And all with a big smile on her face!

Filled with such vitriol, I'm not even sure how I preached

the last message that day. All I knew is that I couldn't wait to get home and make sure Ann felt my wrath. When I walked into the kitchen, there was no "hello" or "how ya doing?" I simply yelled, "I still can't believe you parked in that spot! What were you thinking?"

Ann chirped right back, "I was late getting to church. God gave me that great spot by the front door, and I took it with gratitude."

"God did not give you that spot!" I yelled. We don't yell at each other very much anymore during a fight, but on that day, it was game on!

My youngest son, fourteen-year-old Cody, was sitting at the kitchen table listening to the whole conversation, if you could call it that. I guess he finally had enough because he interjected, "Hey, Dad, don't you and Mom travel around the country teaching couples how to resolve conflict? Is this what you teach them?"

My eyeballs became daggers pointed in his direction, just like in the old cartoons. "You sit right there, son, and I'll show you how to resolve conflict!"

Not missing a beat, I went right back after Ann with more of how I was right and she was wrong. This went on for another ten minutes or so before she finally just walked out of the kitchen and headed upstairs. When she left, I thought to myself, *You* ought *to leave! You know you're wrong and I'm right . . . again!* Honestly, I was so hot that I didn't even want to be in the same room with her at the moment.

Great role modeling for my son.

Yet there was something about her leaving the room that helped me begin to see myself as she was seeing me in that moment. I looked at Cody with an expression that said, *I'm not sure what just happened, but it doesn't look good for either of us.*

Going Vertical

As the room became real quiet—and I mean eerily quiet—I had a moment to think. And in that uncomfortable stillness, I went vertical. All this means is that I came to my senses long enough to invite God to join our situation. Up to that point, I really hadn't cared what God thought, and honestly, I didn't want to know. Yet as I sat there alone with my anger and my self-righteousness (well, I felt alone, but Cody was actually watching me the whole time), I knew I had handled this situation incorrectly. My perspective had failed me yet again, and I needed another one. I knew in my heart that I had heard enough of myself; what I really needed was to hear from God.

So I took a deep breath and asked God to speak to me. I specifically asked him to help me see what I was missing. What I heard from him was short and simple: "Listen." I waited to hear more from Jesus, but that was it. *Really? Just one word?* Yep. *Listen.*

About fifteen minutes later, Ann came back downstairs and stood in the doorway to our kitchen. Cody and I were still the only ones sitting there. She looked at me and uttered words I will never forget: "I go to church every week all by myself because you are there early and you stay late. I do everything around this house because you are constantly working at all your jobs in ministry. I mow the yard. I wash the cars. I snowboard just to be with you and our sons. I wakeboard just to be with you and the boys."

At this point, Cody shot me a look that said, *Dad, I hate to tell you, but you're toast.*

Ann continued. "I cook and clean and wash the cars and take care of this house because you are rarely around! I sit alone in church every week while you stand on stage and preach to the masses. So you know what . . . if I get a chance one time to park by the front door at church, I'm going to take it!"

When I finally listened, I got it. For a few moments, I just sat there. I could feel Cody's eyes boring into my soul, wondering what his "marriage expert" dad was going to say next. I exhaled and then simply asked Ann this question: "Do you feel like Kensington is more important to me than you are?"

She looked down at the floor for a moment and then nodded yes.

Boom. There it was—another monumental moment staring me right in the face. A moment to grab hold of. A moment to embrace. And if I responded humbly and wisely, who knows—perhaps a moment of life transformation.

This was a moment that could change my legacy—and for the first time, I recognized it. As we will discover, these moments are happening all the time in our marriages, but we often completely ignore them because we're not present enough in the moment to ascribe to them the value they are due. We dismiss them as "normal" misunderstandings or conflict, never realizing that real change mostly happens in real life. We envision it happening as it does in the movies, while someone is scaling a blustery mountain peak or while two too-good-looking-to-be-true actors romantically embrace on the top floor of the Empire State Building.

We often miss the transformations that could be happening today, right here in our own kitchen or right there in that latest text argument between you and your spouse over how late you have to stay out again tonight. Going vertical begins with breaking out of the trance of "real" life so you can experience the real change God has for you in those moments. He doesn't need to take you somewhere else to transform you; he has already placed you right where you are. It's a matter of listening through the noise.

Only Half the Truth

God told me to listen, and what I was hearing changed everything. He was speaking to me about my life and my priorities through Ann. In the past, I would have argued with Ann about how she felt. I would have told her that she was obviously my highest priority and that she was wrong for feeling anything other than that. In my heart, I truly believed that Kensington wasn't nearly as important to me as she was.

But we weren't dealing with just *my* heart. I was not authorized to define reality for both of us, no matter how much I felt that I was. The truth also contained what was going on in *her* heart as well. Until I acknowledged that, I didn't really have the truth; rather, I only had my half of it. And everyone knows that half-truths are not really true.

The truth was, what she was feeling in that moment wasn't fiction, as I had treated it; it was reality. It really didn't matter what *I* thought. Ann was feeling neglected, and that was her reality. And her reality was a key part of my reality, even if I didn't know it. I could defend my position until the cows came home, but the position that needed to be acknowledged was not mine; it was *hers*.

I needed to deal with her reality as the truth.

Cody was watching as this whole epiphany unfolded within me, and in retrospect, I'm really glad he was there to witness it. I stood up and made my way across the kitchen floor. I took Ann into my arms and said, "Ann, I'm truly sorry for yelling at you today. I'm sorry you feel that my job is more important to me than you are. You are more important to me than anything else in my life apart from God, but if you don't feel that way, then that means I'm living this out wrongly. You're right, I *am* too busy with Kensington, and I need to look at my schedule and make adjustments to reflect my priorities. Would you sit down with me today so we can look at these things together?"

Yep, there went my nap—but it was a small price to pay.

Parking Spot Epiphany

I realized in that moment that this argument was never about a parking spot; this was about Ann feeling loved by me. Feeling cherished by her husband. Her number one need is to feel loved by her husband, and I had failed her—and had been failing her—for quite some time. The parking spot was what God used to show me how completely insane my schedule had become. I had been reciting what every Christian man says about his priorities: *God first, family second, and job third.* How many times have you heard that sequence being preached from the rooftops in every Father's Day sermon, men's conference, and small group curriculum?

In my case, the truth was that these had become nothing more than words. These were not the reality I was living. I always preach that you can tell a man's priorities by looking in two places—his wallet and his calendar. Where we spend our money and what we do with our time always trump the words we say. Whenever I'm sitting with a married couple and the husband begins telling me how important his wife is to him, I stop looking at him and discreetly glance over at his wife to see how her demeanor reacts to his idealistic declarations. She will either nod in agreement with him, confirming that what he is saying actually is her reality, or she will subconsciously stare at the floor—or perhaps even consciously roll her eyes—which indicates that his words on this matter are meaningless.

I was that husband whose words produced the second reaction—and I didn't even know it. I could preach it well, but I wasn't living it. Going vertical in this moment meant I needed to hear what God was saying to me about this particular situation. Yes, I know that being aware in the moment is the hardest part, but it's also where the greatest potential resides for God to make something incredible out of something horrible.

Loving and Cherishing

As husbands, God has called each of us to "love your wives, just as Christ loved the church and gave himself up for her" (Ephesians 5:25). I have found that this word *love* often doesn't mean as much to us men as it should. Think about it: we say we love all kinds of things. *I love chocolate milkshakes. I love my Harley. I love the Super Bowl . . . that my beloved Detroit Lions will actually play in someday.*

So when Paul commands us to love our wives, we really don't know what that means. Something that helps me is to replace that word with another word that we men do understand: *cherish* (which is the actual word used in some English translations of verse 29 of Ephesians 5). If *cheer* makes a man feel respected, then *cherish* makes a woman feel loved.

Now that's a word we can relate to because we are actually pretty good at cherishing things. To cherish means to protect. To pamper. To polish. To provide whatever is needed. We take care of our most "cherished" possessions. I have played guitar since I was eight years old, and I have a collection of several guitars and basses. I cherish (protect, polish, pamper) each one. I keep them in a room with proper moisture so they don't warp. As a *picker*, I am very *picky* about who gets to touch my guitars. I treat them like they are my babies. I know men who do the same thing with their TVs, their golf clubs, or their motorcycles.

By the way, I cherish those things in my life as well.

But let's be honest, the idea of cherishing these temporal things should only be a starting point for understanding marriage. It should open our eyes to the absolutely radical way we are called by God to love our wives, who are so much more infinitely valuable than some pile of metal, rubber, and electronics.

That day I began to explore what it would look like for me to cherish Ann like Christ cherishes the church. Not just convince *myself* of how much I loved her in my heart, but to really love her in a way that *conveyed* love to *her*. To date, I am still in the process of exploring that—as we will all do for the rest of our lives. But I did find out in my kitchen that day that one huge way to really communicate "I love you" to Ann was to spend time at home with her and our boys.

Every man and woman is different, but Ann's top love language is time. She spells love *T-I-M-E*. She wants time with me while nothing else is distracting my attention or affection. This means that when we're on a date (or even just talking together in the kitchen), she wants me to put away my phone, which includes actual phone calls, but also voice mails, emails, social media updates, and the latest scores from the latest game happening right now. And yes, I said the word *date*. Married couples need to continue to date. And they need to date each other every week.

I can hear certain husbands (as well as certain wives) complaining, "Every single week? Seriously?"

You try to play golf every week, don't you? Or ride your bike? Or work out? Or clean the house? Or watch your favorite show? You see, whatever we value the most, we find—no, we *make*—time to do. In this case, can you guess what (or more accurately, who) is most valuable in your home? Your spouse. If he or she walks out, then there will be no home left to speak of anymore.

Right then and there in that kitchen, I decided that to the best of my ability, Ann was never again going to have the reason to feel that my job (or anything else) was more important to me than her. In our case, the first step to cherishing her more dearly was to begin pruning my calendar so that I could better protect my time to pamper my wife.

The second step was dressing up and heading out on a much-needed date together that very Sunday night—it was *so* much better than a nap. And finally, I was becoming a man (and in my case, an actual preacher) who was practicing what he preaches.

Regarding the parking spot of ill repute, I never again saw Ann take the front spot. But even if she had, I wouldn't have balked.

Nothing—not even the premier parking spot—is too good for the one I cherish the most.

PART THREE

Intimacy

Twelve

SEX IN
the Chapel

The more than thirty years that Dave has served as the chaplain of the Detroit Lions have given us many great stories to tell. His time with the team is not always just about the players themselves or winning games, but also about their marriages and families. This means we often work together to serve them in many areas of their lives—including sex.

It shouldn't be a secret or at all taboo to acknowledge that sex is an integral part of any marriage, and yet people—even married people—often avoid talking about it at all. They choose instead to bury their feelings, addictions, perceptions, and insecurities, hoping that everything will just magically work out if they simply leave this topic alone.

But when it comes to sex, we need to be talking—a lot.

When people are willing to be vulnerable and open up about sex, amazing things happen. At one of the Bible studies Ann leads for wives of Lions players, a woman mentioned that it was her husband's birthday, and he was taking her out for dinner and a night at a hotel. This was a wife whose husband had never come to the weekly Bible study that Dave does with the guys.

"And what are you doing special for him?" Ann asked.

She sheepishly replied, "Well, I'm going with him."

Ann said, "You need to do something special for him since it's his birthday. How about going to a lingerie store and picking out something sweet he will love?"

The wife replied, "Uh, that's not really me. I've never done anything like that before."

"Go on, it will be fun!" Ann insisted. So off she went to the store.

The next morning, Ann got a call from this wife who excitedly said, "Ann, last night was incredible! My husband said it was the greatest night of our marriage. And then he asked me where I got this idea to wear lingerie. I told him the idea came up at Bible study. He said I should never ever miss that Bible study!"

And guess who showed up at the Lions' couples study the next week? Yep—Mr. Happy Husband. He was now interested in God. In fact, six weeks later, he gave his life to Jesus, and today that couple serves in full-time ministry. Amazing!

And it all started with some lingerie.

Sex is a good thing in marriage; in fact, it is a *God* thing. Why should we think it odd that God would use a conversation about sex to open the door to the gospel? We shouldn't think it odd, because enjoying God's design for sex can go a long way to changing marriages and lives.

Let's Talk about Sex

Several years ago, we were asked to speak about marriage on the Love Like You Mean It Marriage Cruise. At first, we didn't know what topic they wanted us to address. About six weeks before the cruise, I texted Bob Lepine, *FamilyLife Today*'s radio host and the cruise director, and asked him what topic he would like us to speak on. After several back and forth texts about possible options, Bob texted back that he would like us to talk about sex. I texted back, "Are you sure you want a couple in their fifties talking about sex?" He replied, "Are you still having sex? Then stop long enough to talk about it!" I'm still laughing at that comment.

And in case you are wondering, yes, we still have sex, and it's time to do some talking about it. When we address this topic at our marriage conferences around the country, we often see a line of couples wanting to talk with us afterward. We expect them to tell us how beautiful this part of their marriage has become, but tragically, we often hear the opposite. These couples use the short amount of time they have—even if it's only thirty or forty-five seconds—to reveal various details of the issues they have in their sex lives. Some might say they share a little too much.

Through tears, we hear from men and women alike who share that they were molested as children and that they've never told anyone until now. We hear from husbands who have been caught viewing porn—yet again. Married couples who have not had sex in months, years, and sometimes decades. Women and men who tell us that they have not told their spouses that they had dozens of sexual partners before they got married. Husbands who feel that they have to have sex with their wives several times a day, and if they don't get it, they masturbate several times a day instead. Wives who have asked us if their husbands are guilty of raping them. Husbands and wives who ask if they should tell their spouses about their affairs. Christian couples who wanted to know if they should keep viewing porn together. And keep in mind that these are often church-based conferences.

When we speak to live groups, we always have fun around this topic, because there is so much to joke and laugh about. But the honest truth is that we're often hurt and wounded in this area, and we carry around so much junk. So many of us are struggling silently because our sex life is horrible and we can't even talk about it, even with our spouses. The struggle and the silence can devastate our marriages and our very lives.

This is why we think you should learn to talk about it.

Sex has been one of the greatest joys of our marriage, but it's also been one of the most difficult areas of our marriage. Over the years, we've faced countless struggles to understand one another in the bedroom. Understanding *her* needs. Understanding *his* needs. Understanding conflicting desires related to frequency—how many times a week, a year, or even a day. We have fought about this. We have cried about this.

So if you are struggling in this area, you are not alone. Not at all.

The thousands of people who have approached us with these stories—they are you! They are us. We grew up in church, but for most of our lives, the church was silent on this topic. It was never talked about. If you ever heard anything about sex from anyone in the church, especially from a pastor, you were made to think that it was really wrong, that God was against it, and that you might go bald if you do it. I guess they were right on the bald part—and Dave is really bald, if you get what we're saying.

But we all know that people are struggling with all kinds of sex issues, and the culture is talking about sex nonstop. It's in our faces every second. You can't watch the Super Bowl halftime show or even a Hardee's commercial without something sexual happening. No wonder our kids—and, let's be honest, ourselves—often don't quite know what to think about sex.

Let's explore both God's perspective and the human perspective on the matter. Let's take a look at God's beauty and human brokenness.

Becoming Comfortable with the Sacred Beauty of Sex

God designed sex: "So God created mankind in his own image, in the image of God he created them; male and female he created them. God blessed them and said to them, 'Be fruitful and increase in number; fill the earth and subdue it'" (Genesis 1:27–28).

Who is the main character in this story? The protagonist? The one initiating toward the others? God. It was God who created Adam and Eve, put them in the garden, blessed them, and told them to be fruitful and multiply. At that point, sex became a very real—and godly—part of the creation story. God himself created sex, even commanding the first husband and wife to enjoy it.

When we were back in seminary, we asked the question, "From God's perspective, what is the primary purpose of sex?" And often we concluded that there was one purpose, that is, *procreation*. This was the church's messaging for decades—you should never have sex except for the purpose of reproduction. But this is not scriptural. Procreation is one of the purposes, but it isn't the only one.

Besides procreation, the other two purposes for sex are *oneness* (or intimacy) and *pleasure*. To highlight this point, Dave sometimes jokes with our church staff, saying, "God wants us to have sex on the days that start with the letter T. Tuesday, Thursday, Today, Tomorrow, Tadurday, and Tunday!"

All kidding aside, let's first address the purpose of oneness. When a person has sex, whether in marriage or even in a one-night stand, a soul connection occurs. Even when emotional intimacy seems to be distant from the experience, the fact remains that God designed sex to be the most intimate, beautiful act in which human beings could ever engage. There is such a depth of intimacy that it is beyond physical.

Sex is soul intimacy.

And yet today, if you talk to people from high school ages to adulthood, there is a generally flippant attitude about sexuality. It really doesn't matter if "I love him" or in some cases even if "I like her"; it's just a physical act done for pleasure. But God made it to be so much more! This flippancy is why we are so scarred. We are so wounded because sex is not just a physical act, but rather something that affects our very souls, which is why it can also be extremely hurtful.

God created our psyches to bond with the psyches of those with whom we are intimate. In sex, chemicals are released that foster intimacy and oneness, something that is designed for and is crucial to the covenant of marriage. That is why engaging in sex with someone outside of the marriage context can be so destructive.

As anyone who has ever had sex knows, sexual pleasure is virtually unmatched by any other experience. God designed the human body in such an incredible way that when a man or woman reaches sexual excitement, nerve endings release a chemical into the brain that is much like a drug high (not that I know anything about a drug high!). This "high" can be addictive, just like a drug. Obviously, that can lead to many negative choices when it comes to sex, but it also can result in a unique bonding between a husband and wife. This pleasure makes us want to come back for more, and that "coming together" actually bonds us in a deep and beautiful way as husband and wife. This means that a married couple is literally bonded together as one both physically and chemically by God as they have sex. Wow!

It's almost as if every time we make love with our spouse,

we are renewing our marital vows of bonding together, until death do us part. That's the beauty of God-ordained sexual pleasure mixed with the covenant of marriage. Only a good good Father could come up with that.

Sex is not only for bonding, but for pleasure too. I don't know if you've noticed this yet, but sex done right actually feels good—really good. And that is a gift from our Creator. He designed us to experience great pleasure when having sex. Think of it in the way someone once said it to us: "Only God could create an act so pleasurable that when you do it, you sometimes yell his name out loud." I hope you are laughing right now because that is funny!

Such talk of the godly pleasure that can be found in sex seems to make the Pharisee inside each of us squirm just a bit. Perhaps it is because we are so distracted by the counterfeit viewpoints of sex with which we've been inundated by this world or even by the church. It is time that we accept the fact that God is not blushing when sex is either being discussed or being performed according to his perfect design. Actually, we believe that God smiles—and maybe even applauds—when a married couple makes love. Now *that's* a God who is worth getting to know!

The Bible is full of God's thoughts on the matter of sex. Take this passage, for example: "May your fountain be blessed, and may you rejoice in the wife of your youth. A loving doe, a graceful deer—may her breasts satisfy you always, may you ever be intoxicated with her love" (Proverbs 5:18–19).

In the church, when we say *breasts*, people gasp. Her breasts should satisfy her husband? Yes! This is in the Bible. In fact, if you haven't spent much time reading God's Word, you may want to read it more after discovering passages such as these. Song of Songs is literally an R-rated read. It speaks of striptease, oral sex, going out into the garden to fool around, and more—all within a marriage relationship.

If we understood the heart of God, then we would know that when a married man and woman make love, God isn't turning away and saying to himself, *Oh man, there they go again*. No, he applauds. If you can't see a God who would do this, then let us boldly assert that perhaps you don't fully know God in the way he wants you to. Why else would God tell us to be fruitful and increase in number and then give us sex as the vehicle to accomplish these goals? He could have created any other method he so desired to make this happen, from cross-pollination to impregnation by sneezing—the facial tissue industry would explode, by the way.

Instead, he chose this beautiful gift of sexual intimacy, oneness, and pleasure. It is a command from God, not just for the purpose of reproducing people, but also for reproducing a legacy. It is a command because it draws us closer and brings us together. It bonds us in the way God intended. This is why before you're married, the enemy will do everything in his power to get you to have sex, but after you're married, he will do everything in his power to keep you from having sex.

If there is ever an area of marriage in which we need to invite the vertical perspective, it is into our sex lives. Otherwise, sex becomes all about us. And then something God uniquely designed to help, heal, and bond us together becomes instead something that damages, wounds, and drives us apart.

Spice It Up!

We believe that when we invite God into our bedrooms, everything changes for the better. His perspective invites us to be free to enjoy married sex the way he intends. This can help us find joy again under the sheets—or anywhere else for that matter.

It's time to spice it up a bit. Far too many couples fall into a dull, boring routine when it comes to their sex life. Right side of the bed. Left side of the bed. C'mon, get a little creative!

A few years back, Dave was speaking to the Detroit Lions football team at their weekly chapel service in the team hotel before a home game. It was actually his birthday that day, and we were going out for dinner after chapel. As Dave was up front addressing the more than thirty players and coaches in attendance, a player walked in a few minutes late. He walked right to the front row and before sitting down handed Dave an envelope that read, "For Dave Wilson. Emergency. Open Immediately!"

At first, the letter didn't register with Dave because he was in the middle of his message. He figured that whatever it was could wait for just a few short minutes. So he put the envelope down and kept talking. But the player immediately said, "Dave, this can't wait. You need to read that letter right this minute!"

Suddenly Dave understood what was happening. Thinking that something terrible might have happened with the kids or Ann, he quickly ripped open the envelope and, out of panic, began reading the note out loud. That's when he read the following words in front of all the guys: "Hey, big boy, come get your naked birthday present lying on the bed in room 3136. I'm up here waiting for you right now. You better hurry."

Dave then realized what he had just read—out loud for all to hear. He looked up to see every guy in the chapel staring at him with their jaws dropped. They couldn't believe what they were hearing. Dave regained his composure and said, "Well, guys, I guess you know where I'm going as soon as I'm done with you."

At that moment, Bobby Ross, Lions head coach at the time, said, "You better go right now, Dave. We'll take it from here." And with that, Dave ran out of the room, ripping off his clothes as he ran toward the elevator!

To this day, players still tell him they will never forget that particular chapel. They comment that Dave's birthday letter modeled for them how a deeply spiritual marriage has a deep and creative sex life as well.

So go ahead and spice it up a little! Bring back some fun and joy to your bedroom. Speaking of bedroom, that isn't the only place you can make love. Get a little creative. We'll just say that at our house we have a trampoline . . . and a back deck . . . and a Harley Davidson. Okay, the Harley has just been one of our fantasies, but we're not telling whose.

Okay, now you can stop blushing. This chapter is done.

Thirteen

DON'T YOU THINK ABOUT SEX
All the Time?

It was one of those days. You know the kind. Instead of instantly waking up with joy and anticipation of all that lay ahead, I (Ann) needed a pulley system to pry open my eyes. As the light invaded my space, several realities made themselves abundantly and painfully clear: I was having that first morning sickness feeling of pregnancy; my two-year-old was lying in his bed letting off the screams of a banshee scorned; and my four-year-old was tugging at my arm, reminding me—along with the screaming—that it was morning and he was hungry.

Ugh . . . yes, it was *that* kind of morning.

Dave was working at home that day, writing a sermon with his feet propped up on the desk and his Bible on his lap. I casually glanced at him as I passed by on my way to the boys' room to make beds and collect dirty clothes. CJ was throwing pillows at Austin, who was yelling at CJ in retaliation—and they both began running around me in circles, yelling at each other. I hadn't showered yet, hadn't dragged a brush through the matted mess of my hair—heck, I hadn't even brushed my teeth yet.

After I finished in the bedroom, I passed back by Dave's office and glanced at him again. That's when it happened—again. Jealousy, envy, pity—they all simultaneously hit me full force. *Wow, it must be nice to get to sit alone all by yourself reading the Bible. His life is so much easier than mine! I can't even remember the last time I uttered a complete sentence without scolding or correcting—or the last time I had a good night's sleep, for that matter.*

I didn't say any of these things out loud, but the budding feelings of discontent were planted and had started to take root.

Thunk!

Austin finally connected his fist with CJ's back, and now both were crying—*sigh, again.* Mom back to the rescue, or at least to the mediation. I put the dirty clothes in the laundry basket and plopped Austin right up on top of the clothes—he probably wondered if he was going to join the clothes in the washer. My pregnant belly was starting to protrude, so as I picked up the basket, I had to hold it down below the rising bump. CJ followed beside me and the little Moses I had in my basket as we all headed out of the room and into the hallway. As I passed by Dave's office, I glanced at him again, and those familiar feelings returned.

"Hey, Ann, wait a minute!" Dave called out from his office.

I paused with hope. Did he want to encourage me—and perhaps even join me—in my mundane chores? Had he noticed how hard I was always working and wanted to thank me for my tireless effort? Had he had a stirring in his heart from God and now realized I was by far the very best thing that had ever happened to him?

My eyes locked with his in anticipation of the trophy of words he was about to reward me with. Here it comes . . .

"Do you think about our sex life all the time?" he asked innocently.

No, there was no way he just asked that. Perhaps a clump of dried earwax or Play-Doh had nestled into my ear canal. The boys were whining to get moving, so I said, "Everyone, be quiet, so I can hear Dad! Now, what did you say, Dave?" My heart was expectant but trembling, hoping I had merely misunderstood him.

"Don't you just think about our sex life all the time?" His legs dropped off the desk as he turned his chair toward me, sporting a sexy look and a glint of hope in his eye.

Now, I know you may (or may not) be thinking, *Wow, how cool is it that he's thinking about you like that! You're a lucky girl. You must be a little tiger in the bedroom!*

Uh, no.

Yes, I was glad my husband desired me sexually. This is a gift that shouldn't be dismissed or diminished.

Now as to the matter of the "tiger," I again say . . . uh, no. In that moment, I was more like a tired old goat that had just scaled Mount Kil-A-Libido (sound it out). I was in that phase that left me feeling as if nothing on my body belonged to me or was the same after three pregnancies. I was living on the hellcat hormone roller coaster.

Then there was Dave.

"Are you serious right now?" I asked, as tears began to form in my eyes. He obviously didn't see them yet.

"Yes! I'm just sitting here thinking about our sex life, and I just realized that I think about it *all* the time!" He said this as if such a revelation would propel our sex life to new heights.

I didn't have anything left, so I just let it all out. "Look at me, Dave! Do I look like I've just been flitting about the house daydreaming about our sex life?" Then I burst into tears.

I suppose that was the first time that morning that Dave had truly looked at the scene before him. Hair disheveled, eye goo still encrusted, baggy sweatpants, and some sort of breakfast food still fresh on my sweatshirt. Yep, that is the beautiful reality of being married and having kids.

With his dreams of a late-morning rendezvous shattered, he looked down, swiveled his chair back into place, and kicked his feet back onto his desk.

"Bummer," he muttered.

I let out a deep sigh as I resituated my laundry basket (and child) and trekked back down two sets of stairs to the basement laundry room. All the while, I was thinking, *How can we be so different? How can he not understand the world I live in? Will we ever be on the same page again sexually—especially since I'd rather slug him than sleep with him?*

I sent up a prayer to God in desperation, honestly not really expecting him to answer it. It went something like this: "God, please help Dave to understand what it's like to be me!"

I guess God overlooked the fact that I didn't expect him to answer because, let me tell you, he answered in an incredibly effective way.

Fast-forward two months, I went into early labor and was put on bed rest for five months. Couple that with the fact that we were in the midst of taking the biggest risk of our lives in starting Kensington Church. Our world was in chaos, and yet I had to focus on taking care of the little one who was still to arrive.

As I was now forced to rest, Dave courageously took on the domestic tasks, including shuffling baskets of kids and clothes and whatnot through the house. He became a full-time mom during the day and a full-time pastor at night, catching up on all his work for the church when the kids were in bed.

Several times as he frantically moved from one chaotic moment to the next, he would pass by our room where I would be lying down reading my Bible or a book, just peacefully incubating and meditating, because that's what I had to do.

After one particularly long and exhausting day, Dave collapsed into bed next to me and let out a huge sigh. "It's been one of those days!" he lamented. He began to recount all the things he'd had to do and the frustrating circumstances he had tackled head-on. Mom-like exhaustion began to take its toll on him, even as he was speaking. His words started to mingle together like gibberish, and his eyelids began an involuntary descent.

But just before he drifted off into the kind of sleep only the exhausted can truly appreciate, I leaned in oh-so-close to his ear and softly whispered . . .

"Didn't you just think about our sex life all day long?"

With a mischievous grin, he licked his forefinger and lifted his hand in the air, swiping an invisible scoreboard with an imaginary "1." "Touché!" he whispered.

Frequency (and Infrequency)

Have you ever wondered why God made men and women so different? These differences reveal themselves in many areas of marriage, but in our marriage, nothing has brought them to the surface more than sex. I cannot overstate how much Dave and I have struggled in this area over the years.

I wonder if you can relate.

In our early years of marriage, we thought, *Wow, this is easy! Why are all these couples whining about their sex lives?*

Time, romance, and togetherness were abundant in those days—the ingredients that make the perfect recipe for success in the bedroom. But then it happened—children! We were ecstatic to discover that I was pregnant. We even vowed to never let pregnancy and babies disrupt our romance.

But then reality set in: how the presence of little underdeveloped humans in your house—and often in your bed—disrupts not only your romance but also every other detail of your lives, from sleeping to eating to going to the bathroom by yourself. Ah, the wonderful miracle of the very best days—and the hardest days—of your life.

The result was that Dave and I found ourselves fighting continually about sex. He was frustrated by the frequency—or perhaps I should say, the infrequency. One time I asked him how often he would like to be having sex. Without hesitation, he replied, "Every single day!"

I laughed out loud and then quickly interjected, "Well, that's *not* going to happen!"

With a disappointed frown and a sullen anger simmering just below the surface, he asked, "Well, how often do *you* want to have sex?"

He had really opened up Pandora's box with that one. I wanted to reply, "Hmm, when you start helping me with the kids more, help around the house more, rub my back once in a while, and tell me how awesome I am, maybe *then* I'll think about having sex on those days."

But I simply replied, "Two days a week, maybe less?"

We can get into trouble by offering up target numbers on this topic. It's all too easy for people to begin comparing their sex lives to that of others. We can get bent out of shape for no reason, feeling bad or good about the frequency of making love. But in that moment with my husband, I was just trying to find some middle ground.

The point was that we just couldn't seem to find a balance. Dave continually felt neglected sexually, and I continually felt neglected relationally. I came to realize that I wanted sex when I felt good about our relationship—when I felt like Dave and

I were on the same page and connecting emotionally. Dave, on the other hand, didn't need any of that to have sex. Even so, once we had made love, he did seem to suddenly open up, become more affectionate, and be just all around happier and more helpful.

It seemed like we were totally missing each other—and yes, we each expected the other person to make the first move to correct the problem.

Loaded Down with Luggage

One night I was praying about this—well, let me rephrase that. One night I was *venting* to God about how frustrated I was with Dave and the fact that he and I were so different in the area of sex. I often see and understand things through pictures or visuals, and that night, I drew a mental picture of how Dave and I approach sex in such different ways. The picture that came into my head was that of luggage.

To understand it better, let me illustrate it personally. Let's imagine that I give Dave *that* look—you know, that look that says, "Hey, hottie, how 'bout tonight?"

Well, whatever Dave is doing at the time is like a piece of luggage he is carrying. When Dave is watching a football game, the piece of luggage called "sports" is in his lap. In my experience, men tend to pick up one piece of luggage at a time. In Dave's case, this means he only opens one piece of his life at a time.

This explains why Dave and I could have just had the biggest fight of our lives and resolved it, and then two seconds later, he can put the conflict bag down, pick up the piece of luggage marked "sex," and be absolutely ready to go. To him, it's as easy as swapping bags.

So when Dave gets "the look," there is now only one thing on his mind: sex. He picks up that bag called "sex," and nothing can drive that bag out of his hand—well, except sex. A 9.9 earthquake could be shaking the whole globe, but he would still be holding on to sex—and could probably even be having sex—during the global catastrophe. "The look" cues Dave to go upstairs to our bedroom, climb into bed, and hope against all hope as he clutches to his sex suitcase.

Me, on the other hand—picture me downstairs at the end of a long day, a mom with three busy children, a part-time job, and countless other responsibilities. You see, as a woman, I don't generally pick up one suitcase or bag at a time.

I carry them all at the *same* time.

As Dave is upstairs with a singular focus, I'm downstairs with multiple focuses. And generally, something like this is going through my head:

"Okay, what should I make for breakfast tomorrow morning? Do we have any milk left? I need to pack lunches for the kids before I go to bed." You see, I've picked up the cooking and food suitcase.

"Austin seems to be getting a bad cold and is really congested—maybe he shouldn't have milk in the morning because that seems to make his congestion worse. Also, he was complaining about his ear hurting. I wonder if he has an ear infection. Maybe I should call the doctor in the morning and make an appointment, just in case." I just picked up the nursing suitcase.

"I better clean up the house now so I don't have to pick up in the morning. It looks like the dishwasher is full, so I better turn it on and let it run a cycle. Gosh, I haven't dusted in weeks!" There's the cleaning suitcase.

"CJ has football practice tomorrow—did I get all of his stuff washed? What about Dave's shirt that he needs ironed for the event this weekend?" Now I'm carrying the laundry suitcase.

"I just saw my Bible sitting on the bench. Oh Lord, I'm so behind in my Bible reading, and I still need to prepare for the Bible study I'm leading in two days." Cue the picking up of the spiritual suitcase—plus the guilt suitcase for not spending enough time with God.

"I can tell that Mom and Dad are disappointed that I haven't called more. I need to call them and see how they're doing—I do love and miss them so much." Now I've picked up the daughter suitcase.

"Austin seemed like he was sad tonight. I need to spend some more time with him this week to see what's going on." The psychologist suitcase.

"Okay, time to go upstairs, brush my teeth, and wash my face—oh, now I'm noticing these new wrinkles. Ugh. Put on these pajamas—it looks like I'm gaining weight in my stomach. Note to self: do a better job of eating healthily and get to the gym more often." Now I've picked up my "compare myself to the most beautiful and the skinniest women of the world" suitcase.

Finally, I look at the clock only to realize that it's almost midnight, so I tell myself to do a better job tomorrow with time management—which, by the way, is my "better organize myself and my family" suitcase.

By the time I climb into bed, I have at least ten different suitcases all strapped to my brain. Each one is heavy, and I simply can't stop thinking about everything at once—oh, that's right, Dave is here too.

Dave gives me "the look"—the one I gave him, like, five hours ago. His version of "the look" says, *Where have you been? I've been up here waiting for you all night with my one little suitcase!* Of course, by this time I've totally forgotten that I had given Dave "the look" in the first place. I usually end up thinking to myself, *Maybe, Dave, if you wouldn't be so selfish and think only about yourself, I would have been up here earlier!*

Yep, that particular suitcase needs a bellhop, and yet, I lay it right over my heart—it's the "resentment and self-pity" suitcase.

Dave leans over and places his hand on my stomach. "What do you think?" he purrs in my ear. "Is this happening tonight?"

I inwardly moan because I am physically and emotionally drained, exhausted by all that I have done and still have left to do. Can't he understand that I'm carrying a luggage rack of suitcases here!

"Honey, I'm so tired. Can I take a rain check for tomorrow night?"

Dave rolls over to his side of the bed, throws his little sex suitcase on the floor with an angry huff, picks up his sleep suitcase, and drifts off to sleep.

And now I have just added a twelfth suitcase to my already mounting pile—the marriage guilt bag. I lay it across my face as tears pool into my eyes—the weight of this bag is suffocating. Now I can't sleep, even though I'm so exhausted. I really want to have a great sex life like we used to, but all this luggage seems to be growing heavier each year, and I just don't know how to simply put them all away during sex.

Just as if twelve real suitcases were piled on our bed, these always seem to get in the way and leave little room for anything romantic to occur.

I feel like God gave me this visual to explain to Dave how women carry such heavy loads. I have used this countless times at marriage conferences to demonstrate to men why we women can struggle in this area. It's not that we don't like sex, but rather that we are overwhelmed with life and the heavy burdens we lug around.

I haven't even mentioned until now the lifelong suitcases of sexual abuse or other sexual baggage that countless women carry around. These interfere not only with our sex lives, but with our emotional lives as well.

So back to the question: Why did God make us so different? Why did God make women so complicated? Seriously, it seems that it's way easier to be a man—well, at least in my marriage. Let me interject that some couples find these roles and feelings flip-flopped in their marriage. That's not unusual.

After talking to Dave at length about my frustrations and his resulting frustrations, he looked at me with an expression of relief.

"What does *that* look mean?" I asked.

"I'm just realizing how thankful I am that you're *not* like me. It makes me marvel at the ingeniousness of God."

"I'm not following you," I confessed.

"Think about it. If you were wired the same way I'm wired, we would probably have a lot more sex, but it would only be that—just sex. It wouldn't take very long either. The way you're wired causes us to talk more about our relationship. It helps us go deeper into our feelings and thoughts. You help me as a man to be less self-centered and to concentrate on not just your physical needs, but also your emotional needs. I should stop worrying first about having a better sex life—let's be honest, I need to be a better husband, father, friend, and servant. Your different way of being leads me to work harder to know you and to be affectionate in pursuing you the way I used to—the way you deserve. You are *way* more complicated than me, but you make our relationship reflect the beauty and oneness of God the Father, his Son, and the Holy Spirit."

Jaw drop. I know what you're thinking: *Who thinks like this, right?* But my husband is actually a very smart and godly man. I definitely didn't see that response coming. It made me feel good about God's design . . .

Even though I still think it would be easier to be a man.

Octogenarians and Orgasms

Dave's "miracle response" (as it came to be known) actually reminded me of a small conference we once attended. Howard Hendricks and his wife, Jeanie, were our guest speakers for the evening. Howard has since passed away, but he had a huge impact on Dave and me spiritually. He was an author, a speaker, and a professor at Dallas Seminary. After he had ended his talk that evening, he opened the floor for questions. A middle-aged pastor raised his hand. This pastor had spent a lot of time with Howard, sitting under his teaching at the seminary. Even so, I was surprised at the boldness of his question.

"Prof, what's sex like in your eighties?"

A buzz erupted in the room—a mixture of shock and chuckling at the question and the courage it took to ask something so very personal. Without missing a beat, Howard smiled and loudly proclaimed, "Oh, it's the best it's ever been!"

My first reaction was *ewwwww!* I found his answer to be kind of gross to picture, and yet I was totally delighted by it at the same time. As I looked at Howard, I noticed how much he had aged in recent years from the ravages of cancer and the other debilitating health difficulties that seem to catch up with everyone by their mid-eighties. Jeanie, his wife, was her typical "put together" self—always beautiful, but now also a polished great-grandma.

Howard leaned forward in his chair at center stage to put

on his "professor's hat," teaching us with a hopeful urgency that we would understand truth. "I recently had a young married man approach me after my class asking for help with his sex life. He wanted to know if there were insights about special positions or other pointers I could give him to help him and his struggling new bride. I looked this young man right in the eye and said, 'You kids don't know anything about sex until you've been married fifteen years. Before that, you think it's all about technique or position or how good you are as a lover. After you've been married awhile, you start to realize that God didn't create sex to be about the physical. Sex is about the spiritual—a union of the soul. When you discover *that*, you'll discover great sex!'"

As Howard finished his sentence, Dave and I looked at each other, realizing we had only scratched the surface of God's design for sex in our marriage. We had always thought sex was the culmination of pleasure that ended in climax. It hit me that day that the goal of sex was not orgasm; the goal of great sex was intimacy and oneness.

I'm sure a day may come when because of age, health conditions, or medication that sex will look very different than it does now, but I hope Dave and I will be able to boast that no matter our age, we can have a great sex life, because great sex is a union of the soul!

Let's Get Practical

At this point, you may be a bit frustrated, thinking to yourself, *Okay, thanks for the visuals and the theories, but where do we go from here? What are some practical steps we can take?*

Men, let me encourage you to ask your wife at least once a week, "What's the heaviest bag you're carrying right now?"

It will mean so much to your wife that you care about her life and are willing to engage and help her. In fact, perhaps the next question should be, "Is there a bag I can carry for you that would really help you out?"

Here's one more tip for you men: sometimes we need a little time to drop our bags. When I used the luggage visual to explain how I felt to Dave, even though he better understood my feelings, I could also tell he felt a bit hopeless. If I always carried so many bags and he always carried only one, how were we supposed to find a middle ground? Again, it's important to understand that neither men nor women are wrong in the way they generally carry baggage; they are merely different. I had to stop being angry at Dave for being a man, even if I needed to help him understand ways to better understand the bigger picture of the life I live.

But I did tell Dave that one of the things that might help me put down a few bags was that when I got into bed, if he could just rub my back for even five minutes to help me unwind, it would go a long way toward helping me let go of all my conflicting thoughts.

And gentlemen, stay on the back and don't go any lower unless you are invited to. Not every moment of physical touch has to lead to sex—or else it's all too easy to begin showing affection for what it might do for *you* instead of what it will do for the one you love. At any rate, staying up on the back has always been difficult for Dave—but practice makes perfect, men. You'll get the hang of it.

And for the women, I've heard it said that when it comes to sex, men are like microwaves and women like Crock-Pots. Perhaps there is some truth to this, so at times you may want to try to intentionally turn on the Crock-Pot *before* you go to bed. Start thinking about the evening ahead of time, and maybe even shoot your husband a sexy text telling him you're thinking about him. In other words, make sex one of your important suitcases and not just one that he carries alone. Be intentional and give yourself mental space to consider the intimacy to come as something worthwhile and fulfilling, not just something else you have to carry begrudgingly. A good sex life should be like a warm fire on a cold night—its warmth will draw you close.

So make the effort not to bring every one of your bags to bed every night; that way, you can intentionally draw closer to your husband without having to crawl over a cartful of baggage.

Quick Note to the Guys from Dave

Guys, you may want to read this chapter several times. Ann just gave us a lot of wisdom from a woman's perspective. Sit down and *taaalk* with your wives about this chapter. Become an expert on how she thinks about the sexual relationship in your marriage. Honestly, I was clueless for years . . . and I mean *years*!

I remember Ann saying to me one day in the kitchen after I squeezed her butt, "All you ever want from me when you touch me is sex."

"That's not true," I replied.

She said, "Then why did you just grab my butt? Are you thinking about having sex right now?"

"No!" I insisted. But we both knew I was lying. She then went on to teach me about "nonsexual touch." I honestly had no idea what she was talking about, but I learned . . . and I'm still learning.

Guys, your wife longs to be cherished—remember the chapter about this? She desires you to touch her with a tender affection that communicates nothing more than, *I love you and adore the fact that you are my wife*. If every touch is sexual, then she begins to feel like "a piece of meat" (Ann's words to me). I have learned over the years that holding Ann's hand or putting my arm around her at church makes her feel cherished.

Yes, those nonsexual touches may very well lead to great sex later, but again, this is not the reason you should do it—you should do it because you really do cherish her. Nonsexual touch is foreplay to your wife, just not in the way guys think of it, so don't think that every touch must lead to sex. *Touch her because you cherish her.*

And by the way, when you grab the vacuum cleaner and start cleaning the house, that very well may be perceived as foreplay too! I know, who knew?

Quick Note to the Wives from Dave

I just told your man what foreplay looks like to you. But do you know what really turns your man on? It's not necessarily what you think. When you make the first move sexually, that's a serious turn-on to your husband. This action tells him that you want him . . . and it feels like respect to a man.

Remember, respect is his number one need. I remember a certain afternoon when I was speaking at a meeting with all the staff of our church, about 250 people. As I was looking down at the notes on my iPad, a text from Ann came across the screen: "Hey big boy, you better get home early tonight because I'm going to make this night extra special."

Now when she calls me "big boy," I know where things are headed. I promise that you've never seen a speaker end a session so fast! I said something like, "God just told me, 'That's enough for today.' So session dismissed!" And I raced out of there as fast as humanly possible.

When you initiate sex with your husband—at least once in a while—it communicates that you want him, and that can sometimes be as or more important to men than just saying you love us. This is not because we don't care that you love us; it's just that we usually already know.

I haven't kept any of the "I love you" cards that Ann has given me over the years, but I have every "I want you . . . you are an amazing man" card tucked away in my desk. I know this may seem counterintuitive to women, but it's the way God wired us. While women may feel unloved when their man doesn't *taaalk* with them, share his feelings, or show tender affection, you must understand that when you don't want to have sex with your husband—ever—he can feel just as disrespected. It's that important to your man.

Fourteen

DAVE'S NECK PROBLEM
(Ann's Perspective)

It was the summer of 1981 when I (Ann) first realized that Dave had a serious "neck problem." We were in Daytona Beach with Campus Crusade for Christ during the week that most colleges were on spring break. We had been on staff with their organization for a little less than a year. During spring break, CRU would send students to Daytona for "Operation Sonshine"—to tell other college students (who usually happened to be partying pretty hard at the time) that Jesus loved them and had a plan for their lives.

One of those days, when Dave and I were talking on the beach, I first noted the problem. You see, every time a beautiful, scantily clad woman would walk by us on the beach, Dave's neck just couldn't seem to stop twisting and turning to gawk at these girls as they walked past him—and he continued to watch them *all the way* down the beach.

Let me tell you, I was *mad* about it! He was about to have a "wring your neck" problem instead.

"Seriously, Dave! I'm standing right here, and you can't stop yourself from ogling these girls?"

"What are you talking about?" he replied in an innocent tone that I wasn't buying for even a second.

At first, I seriously thought he was kidding, but I soon realized that this "girl watching" had been such a habit that he didn't even know he was doing it. Of course, you may be of the persuasion that says, *Who cares? Big deal. He's not hurting anyone.*

Well, in this case, you would be wrong—he was hurting *me*!

Like so many women—and many men too, for that matter—I didn't exactly possess the greatest self-esteem when it came to body image. The mirror was not my best friend. Because of this, every time Dave went all "go go gadget neck" in my presence, it felt as though someone was stabbing a knife in my chest. And speaking of chests, I could also hear a lie being told somewhere in my head, saying, *You know, Ann, if your boobs were bigger, Dave wouldn't want to look at those other women. If you looked better in your bathing suit, he would only be looking at you!*

It was torture for me.

I was only twenty years old, and I so desperately wanted my new husband to only have eyes for me. Outwardly I was angry, but inwardly I wanted to just sit down and cry, because his actions drew all of my insecurities out of their hiding places and into the ugly open air. I went to bed that night trying to turn my mind to anything positive—anything but the shameful thoughts that I had thighs that were too big and boobs that were too little.

My last thought before my eyes fluttered shut were, *Well, Jesus, at least the beach wasn't full of topless girls. Thanks for protecting me from that!*

Little did I know that Jesus probably chuckled at my prayer—you see, he knew what was coming.

Swedish Barbie Dolls

Fast-forward to the summer of 1984 when Dave and I were in our second year of seminary. As part of our schooling, we had to do an overseas internship. We decided to head up a baseball trip, since Dave was the leader of a discipleship program for college baseball players. So we planned to travel in Europe and sponsor baseball clinics, all the while telling other players and fans that Jesus loved them and had a plan for their lives.

As we were making the decision about whether to go, one of the trip's guides asked us if we were aware that we would be doing clinics on a beach in Sweden where 1 to 2 percent of the women would be topless.

That would be a big fact. *No* . . . no one had told us that. However, I reasoned to myself, if it was only 1 or 2 percent, then it couldn't be *that* bad. After all, the guide did say that those few women would be on the most remote areas of the beach.

So off we went to Sweden, Finland, and Germany! We were oh so excited to experience our first mission trip and see what God would do. We landed in Sweden and jumped into cars that would drive us to our beachside housing. As we were driving, the Swedish man in charge turned to us and asked, "Did they tell you that at least half of the women on the beach will be topless?"

Noooooo!

As we pulled up to the beach resort and restaurant, I felt sick to my stomach. I thought to myself, *This is the dumbest mission trip we could ever take! Let's take twenty young men in their late teens and early twenties—all, mind you, who are trying to grow in their relationships with Jesus—and throw them on the beach with a bunch of topless girls and tell them, "Good luck! Now go tell everyone about Jesus!"*

All twenty of us entered the little beach restaurant where

a meal had already been prepared for us. It was a cute little room with doors that opened right out onto the beach. The guys were hungry, and we were all tired from our trip. The food was delicious, and the room was filled with anticipation of what this leg of our trip had in store. I was facing the door that opened out toward the beach, and I had an incredible view of the crystal blue water and white sand.

Then it happened. The doorway was suddenly filled with three drop-dead gorgeous, long-legged, buxom beauties. Barbie and her two companions were actually real, live beings—and some kid out there forgot to put their bikini tops on!

The room was instantly quiet—you could have heard a pin drop. I glanced around our table to find that jaws were literally hanging wide open . . . and there may or may not have been drool pooling on the tabletop.

Then suddenly, I remembered my twenty-six-year-old husband sitting next to me, and a rush of fear gripped my heart. I whipped my head around to look at him. The state in which I found him was almost sad—his head was bowed as low as it could possibly go without falling off altogether. He was also shoveling food into his mouth as if he had never eaten before. I was instantly—albeit temporarily—relieved that his neck problem had not had a sudden flare-up in this exact moment.

To encourage him, I leaned over and sweetly whispered in his ear, "If you lift your head for even one second, you are a dead man!"

The Bare-bie triplets happily ordered their drinks at the takeout counter and merrily went on their way back to the beach. After their departure, the room was suddenly abuzz with a renewed excitement among our players—I wonder why.

But the leaders and coaches of the trip seemed a bit disconcerted as they wondered how they would keep these young guys under control and mission minded. I, on the other hand, was overwhelmingly gripped by fear, dread, and anger.

We were assigned our rooms and Dave had to go off to meetings, so I was left alone in our room—alone with God. I was hurt, angry, and fearful that my new young husband would find me lacking. I was the angriest with God. I felt he had betrayed me.

As I paced the room, I yelled out to him, "God, you know all of my fears and insecurities. I've told you countless times that *this* would be my worst fear. I'm afraid Dave will be sorry he married me when he could have someone else more voluptuous and beautiful."

The truth is that as a little girl, I couldn't wait to grow up and look like Barbie. After all, wasn't she the icon—the epitome—of what every woman should look like? I was very athletic and a gymnast for years, but my once-soft curves had grown into hard, sinew-ridden muscle. Instead of transforming into Barbie, I stopped growing and maxed out at five foot one—I was forever destined to be more like Barbie's kid sister, Skipper.

And no one's jaw ever drops when Skipper walks into the room.

As I continued my rant, I felt a small whisper collide with my anger. "Ann, can you trust me?"

"No! I *can't* trust you! That's pretty obvious right now!"

But as I continued my tirade, the question kept coming to my mind over and over again. It was relentless: "Ann, can you trust me?"

Finally, exhausted by my fear, anger, and tears, I fell on my knees before God and cried out, "God, what choice do I have? I will trust you! Please help me. I'm clinging to you as my helper and guide . . . as my Father. I need you not only to help *me* get through this, but to help *Dave* get through this too."

A sense of resolution and strength began to fill my heart, enough that I was able to push the anxiety down a bit. I again tried to take hold of the reminder that Jesus loved me—and that he loved Dave as well—more than I could ever hope for or dream.

A Turning Point

I don't want to sum everything up as if a lifelong problem of fear and anxiety suddenly dissipated after only a short prayer—no, these problems continued, but I had the peace and hope to face them. You see, marriage is a winding story with twists and turns and wins and losses—not a collection of stationary snapshots. We often emotionally treat marriage—and relationships in general—as if each moment of failure or triumph within it is somehow isolated. One bad moment equals a bad marriage, while one good moment equals a good marriage. It all depends on the moment in which we are living, not the whole picture. This is a shortsighted and exhausting way to view your marriage, because the truth is that all relationships experience all of the above. If you try to evaluate based on the ups and downs, you're just asking for relational nausea.

So no, this moment did not completely fix all the other issues in our marriage, but neither should it be dismissed, because something miraculous definitely happened on that trip to the Swedish beaches. In other words, that trip was a turning point of sorts. For the first time, Dave began experiencing some level of success with his neck problem, and for the first time, I started realizing that my worth does not originate, cannot be increased, and certainly is not limited in any way by my physical appearance.

I became more aware than ever of my truest, deepest identity: I am a daughter of the King of kings and Lord of lords—and he is a *very* proud and protective Father. I have been made and equipped to carry out a plan that my heavenly Father uniquely crafted for my specific life. I have been made with a purpose and destiny that both satisfy my soul and reflect the love of Christ to the world. These truths are way more attractive than Barbie or her human equivalents, the Swedish "Bare-bie" triplets.

As I look back on that afternoon some thirty years ago, I chuckle at the insignificance of my dilemma. In retrospect, if that were the most difficult thing I had to deal with, my life would be pretty easy. But we should never minimize the importance of "little" things to our emotional development, to our marriage growth, or to the heart of our Savior to be involved in every facet of our lives. How sweet of God to teach us patiently how to walk with him and trust him with the big things *and* the little things.

In fact, God uses the trust he has forged in us during "little" crises to sustain us in the big ones. Since that trip, I've been faced with actual life-and-death issues related to my own health, the health of our babies, and the death of my very best friend and sister at the age of forty-five.

Time and time again in each of these situations, God asked me the same question he asked me years earlier at that topless beach: "Ann, can you trust me?"

It's never been easy, but I have discovered that yes, *I can trust him*. He is always there. He always loves me deeply. He carries me, and he never leaves me. He comforts me and encourages me to keep my eyes on him—I guess you can say that my eyes tend to wander when uncertainty or crises arise.

It's my own neck problem.

In the book of Proverbs, which is a collection of God's wisdom for practical living, Solomon writes, "Trust in the LORD with all your heart and lean not on your own understanding; in all your ways submit to him, and he will make your paths straight" (Proverbs 3:5–6).

God calls us to completely trust him and his ways in our lives. Think about your own marriage. Does it work out well when you trust your spouse with "some" of your heart? It doesn't work out well with God either. God invites us out to that scary place of complete trust. It's like leaning out over a cliff with nothing but a rope holding you back—you can't fully understand the strength and safety of that rope until you release *all* of your weight to its tension. You can talk about the power of that rope. You can sing songs about that rope. You can memorize statistics about that rope. But until you lay yourself out over that cliff, with the danger of death looming before you, and experience the security of that rope, you will never really know.

God is calling us to stop leaning on our own understanding of our versions of the ways we think God should lead our lives. Instead, he keeps asking us, "Do you trust me?" The invitation is to the complete surrender of allowing him to work *his* plan— carried out *his* way—in our lives. His way is so much better than our way, no matter how difficult it may seem at the time. The safest—and also the scariest—place on earth is right in the middle of his plan for you.

Will you trust him with your disappointments? Your fears? Your struggles?

Your marriage?

Your kids?

Your life?

Trusting him is the essence of living vertically.

Fifteen

DAVE'S NECK PROBLEM
(Dave's Perspective)

Ah, the old neck problem. I know it well. Ann's perspective brilliantly reveals how and when this *little* problem of mine first showed up in our marriage . . . and most guys call it "little" in an attempt to cover up the fact that it really isn't little at all.

The problem comes off as pretty simple. I'm a dude, which means I have always enjoyed looking at beautiful women. I still have vivid memories from when I was twelve years old and first began noticing the new curves of my neighbor Sally, who up to that point had always been just another friend down the street.

That friend status changed ever so quickly!

I had never once really noticed Sally or other girls before, but now they had my full attention. Up to that point, playing with the girls down the street was just like playing with boys down the street. But just like Peter Parker, who woke up one morning with a "spidey sense," I woke up one morning with the intense sense that something was now entirely different about Sally—and me too, for that matter. All of sudden, I was feeling things for her that I had not only never felt for anyone else before, but also literally that I had never felt before *at all*. Things in my body were driving these feelings and sensations.

Every single guy on the planet knows exactly what I'm talking about. So from puberty on, I was stricken with what Ann calls my "neck problem." Looking at women as they walked by was something I had never even thought about before this condition was brought to my attention. I didn't know it had taken hold of me, because as far as I could tell, it had taken hold of every other guy I knew too, as if it's just part of being a man.

You see, that's how men often think of this "problem"— that is, their sexual desires—as if "sexual desire" is an irreversible, uncontrollable medical condition for which there is no cure and for which they cannot be held responsible. This is a dangerous way of thinking, because it justifies negative thoughts and actions as if they are harmless, unavoidable, and ultimately inevitable. We begin to consider it a victimless crime of sorts because we aren't thinking of the actual women we are lustfully looking at, but rather only their image, which has conveniently been separated from their value and humanity.

"Come on!" we say to ourselves. "No man can keep himself from lusting after hot chicks. God made me this way!"

This is only half true. God did make us to be sexual individuals, but he did not make us to be unable to control our desires. He has provided for us the Scriptures, his Spirit, and his people to equip us not to be controlled by these desires, but rather to help these desires find their appropriate, fulfilling, and, yes, incredibly fun place within a healthy, passionate marriage.

But so many men wouldn't call it a problem—they just call it biology. However, we were not created to be dominated by biology; rather, we have been empowered by the very Creator of biology himself. We were made to possess self-control, even in this area of our lives.

Denial in Daytona

The truth is that I never once knew I had a problem until Ann pointed it out to me at the beach on our first trip to Daytona Beach. I honestly never realized I was doing it—"it" being straining my neck to turn and drink in with my eyes every scantily clad woman who happened to pass by, even as my wife looked on in shame and insecurity. It had become such a normal part of my life that when Ann confronted me, I denied it. I seriously thought she was crazy and was just overreacting. I rationalized that she was being overly sensitive and was exaggerating my actions to create drama or to get my attention.

Regardless of my protests, she definitely got my attention.

When we left the beach and were back in our room, she let me feel how this "neck problem" hurt her so deeply. She told me how my actions made her feel belittled and ugly. She also told me how she felt embarrassed as other people surely noticed that I was lusting after other women. Ann was a mixture of fierce anger and tears—and it didn't help that I was denying the whole thing. As people often do when they are justifying, I began using definitive language. I said that I "never ever look at other women." Yes, I actually used the word *never*.

Perhaps I was the one who was exaggerating . . . you think?

But I stood my ground, even though she wasn't buying it for even a second. That same evening, we attended a large social gathering, and I decided I would evaluate myself (since Ann's evaluation was obviously not to be trusted) to see if I really looked at other women *that* much. Of course, I knew that Ann would also be watching me as we talked with others in the large room, so this was also my chance to prove her wrong. Besides, none of the women at this event would be in bikinis, like the girls on the beach, so how hard could it be to keep my "man energy" solely focused only on Ann? By the end of the night, I had discovered it was a lot more difficult than I had expected.

I hated to admit it, but Ann was right: I had a neck problem.

A Covenant with My Eyes

Now that my eyes were open not just to the presence of other women, but also to the way I had been looking at those other women, I began to honestly self-evaluate my patterns. Sure enough, it was true that my eyes seemed to naturally follow every attractive woman who walked by or was even in my periphery. Ann was right. Now in terms of her *conclusions* about my wandering eyes, I still didn't agree. I mean, it wasn't like I wanted to have sex with every woman I looked at . . . I wasn't an animal. This train of thought was how I justified my neck problem.

But at that point, I had at least come to grips with the fact that I did indeed take long looks at other women all the time—and not just looks at their faces either; my eyes went up and down their bodies as well.

The whole thing seemed crazy to me because I had never noticed my problem before. Even though I was still protesting Ann's level of protest, I couldn't deny the fact that here I was standing right beside her, knowing she was watching me like a hawk, and yet I still had to fight with all my might to keep my eyes off other women.

The even crazier truth was that I absolutely adored Ann and considered her to be the most beautiful woman I'd ever met. I did not desire to look at other women because I was dissatisfied with our marriage or with Ann—nothing could be further from the truth. Rather I had seemed to develop a really

189

bad habit that I had never confronted before, as I'm convinced most men don't.

You don't have to go to professional counseling to know that the first step in dealing with any problem is to actually acknowledge that you have a problem. That night I took my first step. I admitted to Ann, myself, and God that I had the problem of inappropriately looking at women. My highest desire was to honor Ann and Jesus with my eyes, so I made a commitment to both of them that I would gain control of my eyes.

Job said, "I made a covenant with my eyes not to look lustfully at a young woman" (Job 31:1). That night, I made the same covenant. I was no longer going to let my eyes wander without restraint, staring lustfully at women who were not my wife . . . ever! When I stopped fighting the fact that I had a problem, this solution seemed simpler—I mean, how hard could it be? I was ready to confront my problem and overcome it.

A Pathway to Change

As it turned out, conquering my problem was much harder than I thought it would be. I had been engaged in this pattern for more than ten years and had never once tried to stop because I had never thought I should try. It became evident that if I was going to keep this new covenant, I was going to have to do some serious work in my mind. My wandering eyes and this "neck problem" were merely extensions of my mind.

I had become lazy in my mind, allowing it to dwell on impure thoughts about the women whom I followed with my eyes. I had acted like my "neck problem" was innocent, but the truth was—as it is for most men with the same problem—that I would undress these women in my mind. I would fantasize, even if only for a few seconds at a time, about having sex with them.

I had embraced these kinds of thoughts before marriage, and now I realized I had brought these patterns into my marriage.

It had to stop, and it had to stop *now*!

Many men want to begin the journey to change by simply implementing some discipline or new habit to reverse the old habit. Don't get me wrong, that may be helpful, but the pathway to change does not begin with one doing for oneself what is necessary to change—that is a horizontal approach. What we need the most is the *Vertical*.

I had more than a bad habit; I had a heart that lusted after other women. Yes, this heart loved Jesus and desired to please him—my faults had not negated his grace for me. But I needed that grace now more than ever, not just to forgive me, but also to equip me with the supernatural ability to do more than just avert my eyes, but also to avert my heart.

Good practices are helpful, but they are powerless to transform a heart. But when we acknowledge our need before God and believe rightly about our wrongness and our need for his vertical rightness, then a power higher than our own efforts begins to affect our situation. God does what we can never do, as we should desire and expect him to do. Do we really want a transformation experience that is only as strong as our ability to discipline ourselves? This grace doesn't sound very amazing at all.

So I began by acknowledging my problem and my need for God to transform my heart. I didn't insult him by trying to change myself first and then come to him when my own plan fell short. I came to him as the Source of my change—of *any* change that matters or lasts. No, you may not always feel some huge "aha" in your heart or the complete removal of all temptation when you come to God first, but trust me, when you ask, he will immediately begin the very transformation within you that you can never produce in yourself.

Spiritual Practices

After I began with the Vertical, I could then address the horizontal as well. In my case, I began implementing new practices and disciplines that reflected the heart change I believed God was doing in me. The practice that helped me the most in conquering this habit was Scripture meditation and memorization.

I had always been a student of God's Word, reading and studying it daily, but I had never attacked a specific problem in my life by applying the Bible directly. So I decided to spend the next six months of my life daily memorizing and meditating on the third chapter of Paul's letter to the Colossians. But the real reason I even thought to do such a thing came from what Paul wrote about how God renews our minds:

> Therefore, I urge you, brothers and sisters, in view of God's mercy, to offer your bodies as a living sacrifice, holy and pleasing to God—this is your true and proper worship. Do not conform to the pattern of this world, but be transformed by the renewing of your mind. Then you will be able to test and approve what God's will is—his good, pleasing and perfect will.
>
> Romans 12:1-2

From this passage, we can see that Paul instructs us as believers to no longer copy the patterns of this world. Most men in our world today do not think twice about looking and lusting after women . . . *all* women. This is the pattern of our world: to objectify women as sexual objects rather than see them as people created by God with infinite value apart from their bodies or their ability to satisfy someone's sexual fantasies.

Though it may seem direct and harsh, the practical reality is that our culture considers this way of thinking to be just part of being a man. Our motto has become, "What's the harm as long as I'm just window-shopping?" Paul says we must reject this kind of thinking and choose instead to be *renewed* in our mind—in essence, to choose God's vertical ways above the horizontal thought processes of our culture.

But how exactly is our mind renewed? He answers that question in the first verse: "Offer your bodies as a living sacrifice to God." Paul invokes an Old Testament image of a priest sacrificially killing an animal and offering it as a payment for sin. Paul says, in effect, that we must die to our own desires and instead offer ourselves alive to God. This means giving him everything—even those parts of our lives that are embarrassing to admit, like my neck problem.

We often make concepts like this so spiritual that we fail to even attempt to apply them to "earthly" matters. But take note that Paul specifically uses the term *bodies*. The way you're looking at that girl who walks by your table at the restaurant—offer *that* familiar situation as a sacrifice to God.

And if we will offer such things to him, God will renew our minds through his Word. This is what led me to Colossians 3:1–10, because it is a passage loaded with truth about our minds:

> Since, then, you have been raised with Christ, set your hearts on things above, where Christ is, seated at the right hand of God. Set your minds on things above, not on earthly things. For you died, and your life is now hidden with Christ in God. When Christ, who is your life, appears, then you also will appear with him in glory.

Put to death, therefore, whatever belongs to your earthly nature: sexual immorality, impurity, lust, evil desires and greed, which is idolatry. Because of these, the wrath of God is coming. You used to walk in these ways, in the life you once lived. But now you must also rid yourselves of all such things as these: anger, rage, malice, slander, and filthy language from your lips. Do not lie to each other, since you have taken off your old self with its practices and have put on the new self, which is being renewed in knowledge in the image of its Creator.

I had offered myself to God completely, so now I decided to allow him to renew my mind by memorizing *his way of thinking* instead of mine. So I memorized these ten verses with the goal of meditating on them day after day for more than six months. I ended up doing this for an entire year. Every day, I would wake up and memorize another part of this passage, spending nearly an hour studying and meditating on what this Scripture teaches.

Through this process of believing and submitting my body and will, God began to retrain my mind to dwell on Christ and not on earthly things . . . like other women's bodies. As I immersed myself in his ways, he fulfilled his promise and began to renew my mind. And wouldn't you know it—as my mind and heart began to be renewed and transformed by Christ and his Word, my eyes followed suit.

It didn't happen overnight, but slowly my neck problem began to subside. Six months later, Ann said to me, "Do you realize that you no longer watch women as they walk by?" This moment was a small but very significant victory in my life and in our marriage.

I didn't know it at the time, but that victory wouldn't last.

The Little Black Box

A short four years later, I was named the chaplain of the Detroit Lions professional football team. It was a dream come true. Five years earlier, I had turned down a free agent offer to try out for an NFL team, and now I was becoming the chaplain of another team.

Ann and I had just graduated from seminary in California. So fresh off of receiving my master of divinity, we were moving to Detroit. Within a week of moving there, I was standing on the sidelines at the Lions training camp. Only a few days later, I was boarding the team plane for our first preseason game at Seattle.

All of this was new to me and very exciting.

We landed in Seattle and checked into the team hotel. Rarely had I stayed in a hotel of this caliber—it was a swanky five-star resort. As I picked up my room key, I realized I would be rooming alone because all staff members roomed by themselves. *No problem*, I thought. *This will give me some good time to work on the sermon that I'll be giving to the team at our chapel service tomorrow morning.*

As I stepped into my hotel room and put down my bags, I noticed a little black box on top of the TV. The box had a card attached to it explaining how it worked. It was a digital device for ordering movies—keep in mind that this was 1985. Those boxes are long gone, but that was how movies were ordered back in the day.

I stood in front of the TV and read the card. Basically, there were six movie options: three "Hollywood" movies and three porn movies. As I read the descriptions on the card about each movie, my heart began to pound. I found myself drawn to the porn movies. I had glanced at an occasional *Playboy* or

Penthouse back during my college years, but I had never been strongly drawn to look at anything more than that since then—and certainly I had never watched a porn movie in my life.

Yet there I stood with an ever-increasing desire to check out one of these movies. My heart was literally pounding in my chest. Adrenaline raced through my body as I looked at the card. I knew even as I read the movie summary that these porn movies were off-limits for me. There was no way I would compromise my marriage, my ministry, and my walk with Christ to watch a sex movie.

But then I read the last little paragraph on the card that said the movie would not be added to my room bill unless more than five minutes of it were viewed. Hmm, this meant I could watch up to four minutes and fifty-nine seconds before anyone would know.

That information changed everything.

I turned on the TV. I pushed the button for one of the porn movies. I stood in front of the TV and watched probably thirty seconds of porn, and then I turned it off.

That was it—that thirty seconds changed my life.

My marriage.

My legacy.

My walk with God.

I honestly don't remember what I did next, but it probably entailed falling to my knees and confessing my sin. I walked around the whole evening weighed down with guilt and shame. When I talked to Ann on the phone, I "hid"—and you probably know what I mean. And the whole time, I knew that somehow I had to stand up and speak to the Detroit Lions football team at chapel the next morning, just knowing that I was involved in a cover-up of my sin.

What a way to start my NFL ministry.

The Cover-Up

When I returned home, Ann peppered me with questions about my first road trip in the NFL. She was so excited to hear all of the details, but all I could think about was my sin. I now had a secret.

I had never kept a secret from Ann before. Our marriage was one of complete transparency. We vowed in our dating years to always tell each other everything, no matter how difficult it may be. I was now breaking that vow—there was no way I could tell Ann what I had done. It would crush her, especially since I had conquered my "neck problem" several years earlier. What had I done?

I finally decided that the cover-up was the best I could do because, after all, I was *never* going to do anything like this ever again—or so I thought.

On the next Lions road trip, I walked into my hotel room, and the war began again as if I had never left the first hotel room. As soon as I saw that box on top of the TV, I was engaged in the fight of my life. I honestly could not believe the overwhelming power of my desire to watch porn again. My flesh craved even just another short glance at more female nudity and sex.

After fighting and fighting, I eventually hit that button again, this time watching for forty-five seconds or so. I saw more flesh and more sex acts—and those images became burned into my soul. I again confessed my sin to God and promised to never ever watch anything like that again. This time, I rationalized that it wasn't so bad because I hadn't actually rented a full movie.

I hid again on the phone with Ann—yes, now my secret was growing.

When I came home from that road trip, Ann could sense something was different about me. She asked me several times what was wrong. I simply replied, "Nothing is wrong; everything's great!" But she kept asking until I eventually snapped at her in anger. Now I didn't just have a secret, but I also was telling lies.

I'll spare you the details, but this pattern of sin and cover-up went on for three months. I never rented a movie, but I kept watching a minute or two of porn on every Lions road trip. Oh and of course I would confess my sin and preach a sermon to the team the next morning about how to live as a "man of God."

My heart truly meant it when I repented each time, but I felt like a total hypocrite—because I was.

If that wasn't bad enough, I actually lied about my issue to the men in my accountability group. Every Wednesday morning, I met with my three best friends, and we held each other accountable for living out what we said we were committed to: Jesus, our wives and kids, and our integrity. Above all else, we wanted our lives to match our words. Each week, we would ask each other about our thought lives and any issues of sexual purity we were facing—and especially what we had been looking at. Each week when the conversation came my way, I said, "I'm good! Nothing impure going on with me."

It was nothing but a bald-faced lie.

This pattern festered within me, poisoning my life and marriage with impurity and unbearable shame until finally, after yet another road trip full of sin, I couldn't continue the lie any longer. I broke down and told Ann everything—everything you just read and more.

It was one of the lowest points of my life.

Ann was devastated. She was hurt and angry—*extremely* hurt and angry. She returned to her old feelings of inadequacy, as if my desire to look at porn meant that she was not sufficiently beautiful—or that she wasn't good enough in the bedroom. I told her it had nothing to do with any of that, but of course she couldn't believe me or understand. Heck, *I* didn't even understand.

Then came the anger. Rightly so, she was furious at me for lying to her for months as I covered everything up. She could no longer trust me. Where would this all lead? What other sins had I been covering up? Was this really just happening over the past few months, or had it been going on my entire life?

One broken vow had eroded the foundational integrity of every other vow I had ever made to her.

I wish I could say that once my sin was out in the open, it went away, but it didn't. I still struggled to control this desire, and I often gave in. When Ann would ask me, I would lie again and again and again. Then later, when I couldn't handle the guilt any longer, I would confess everything to her, which made her even angrier that I had lied about it so many times before. Now she saw me not only as a porn addict, but also as a compulsive liar.

Keep in mind that this was all going on *as* we were helping to lead an amazing church that was growing by the thousands each year.

As you might imagine, there were multiple layers to this struggle that I could talk about for years, but suffice it to say that going vertical wasn't just a solitary, simple act. This issue ravaged my life and threatened to destroy our marriage and ministry, but the grace of a vertical God held us together.

Ann and I eventually found victory in our struggle—well, really in *my* struggle. I was liberated from an addiction to porn. Everywhere we speak around the country (and I do mean everywhere), couples approach us and ask for help in this area. Porn and sexual temptation are silent killers in the church, and very few are willing to talk openly about it, much less admit they have a problem.

Honestly, we did not originally plan to spend an entire chapter on this topic, but it felt like God led us here, so we're hopeful that it can help you or someone you know in this intense struggle.

Steps for Dealing with Sexual Temptation

STEP 1: TELL YOUR SPOUSE

If you are struggling with sexual temptation, it's time to come out of the dark and *tell your spouse*. You will not win this battle alone, and as difficult as it feels to do so, bringing it into the light is always better.

It is human nature to hide our sin. We inherit this trait from Adam and Eve in the Garden of Eden. They used fig leaves to cover up their sin; we use all kinds of things to cover up ours. No more hiding. Ask God for help, and then tell your spouse. They may scream. They may cry. They may say, "I wish you had never told me!" Ann did and said all of those things, but she would tell you today that she is glad I had the courage to tell her.

As crazy as it sounds, she trusts me more now than ever, and at least part of the reason is that she knows me inside and out. There is no facade left. There is no mask remaining. She knows me better than any other person on the planet, and this transparency has led to the reestablishment of a greater trust than the one I once destroyed.

STEP 2: GET HELP FROM OTHER PEOPLE

The first step is to tell your spouse, but the second crucial step is to tell someone else *besides* your spouse. Men need to tell another man, and probably more than one. There is safety in the strength and wisdom of groups. This is also true for women—and they will often find even more strength in greater numbers. In other words, men tend to need another man or two, while women often prefer another woman . . . or fifteen!

Obviously, the person you should reach out to *must* be someone of the same gender. You get that, right? You, as a man, should never tell someone else's wife about your sexual temptation. You need someone who understands how difficult your struggle is because they can relate to it.

I remember telling one of my best friends about my struggle. He didn't condemn me, but instead gladly agreed to hold me accountable. Because of his initial kindness and openness, I felt good about letting him in on my temptation as it arose.

However, he didn't ask me about it until six weeks after our first conversation. I realized right then and there that he was not the right guy to hold me accountable. This is an everyday struggle that needs to be dealt with *daily*, especially at the very beginning of your road to victory.

STEP 3: SET UP PROTECTION

Sexual temptation has similarities to all other temptations, and yet it is profoundly different. No other temptation is so relentless. Porn is addictive, and if you allow yourself any access to it, you are going down—no matter who you are or how strong you think you are.

So then, you must take the step to block all avenues of access to your sin. In my house, I cannot watch anything on our cable TV that is rated R or worse. Ann has the parental code for those channels, and she will never let me know what that code is—what a blessing this is! Thankfully, she doesn't struggle with this sin, but we can't act like I don't.

My computer and digital devices all have protective software installed to keep me from being able to access the wrong thing in a moment of weakness. Is this overkill? I mean, am I still that weak? Honestly, I don't want to find out—so I've just cut off the opportunity to find myself in a moment of temptation that I could have avoided. Some you cannot avoid, but many you can.

For the past twenty-five years as a pastor at my church, I have never been alone with another woman other than Ann. I never counsel women alone. I have a window into my office so people can look in at any time. I have had the same assistant for more than twenty-five years, and she and I have never had a meal alone and have never ridden in a car alone. Why the high security? Because I want to be above reproach and never give any room for my flesh to rise up and take me down.

This is an extreme problem, so don't shy away from extreme measures.

STEP 4: EVEN WHEN YOU'RE NOT FALLING, KEEP FALLING ON YOUR KNEES

Yes, it is so important to reach out to God when you have fallen, but let me encourage you to also continue to seek God for strength *each and every day*, even when you are not compromised. You *cannot* win this battle in your own strength—just ask anyone who's tried. It would be so much easier for you if you would believe this and not have to learn it the hard way.

Your walk with Jesus is the vertical foundation for victory in this and all areas of temptation. This isn't a "try harder" kind of victory. You will never win in the Christian life by just "trying harder." You have to lean into the One who has already done the work, allowing your vulnerability before him and before his people to lead you into a lifestyle of being trained wisely, whether through daily spiritual disciplines or just through consistent habits of honest conversations. This is the essence of training ourselves to be godly (see 1 Timothy 4:7).

PART FOUR

Living Vertical

Sixteen

All In

I (Dave) like anniversaries as much as the next guy—well, maybe even more than the next guy. But special moments in our marriage are on a whole different plane of importance to Ann. Ann *loves* to party, making each milestone moment an unforgettable moment. In fact, one of her life mottos is "make a memory"—and there is no one better at doing so. In our house, birthdays are like the Disney parade, complete with fireworks, streamers, and wrapped presents emerging from every empty corner of the house.

Cue our twenty-fifth wedding anniversary. I'm no idiot—even *I* knew this was a big one. I mean, it's a quarter-century, for Pete's sake. This milestone was going to be super significant, so I knew I had to come through in a *big* way for Ann.

I started thinking about it in September, a full nine months before our May anniversary date. One should not dismiss the significance of how early my thought processes went to work. I wanted to surprise her with something extravagant that she would love.

She absolutely loves to travel, so I began brainstorming ways we might be able to fly somewhere extra special, which for those of us who live in the often chilly landscape of Michigan means somewhere warm.

But then my ahead-of-the-game mental process met a familiar foe. The problem with traveling southward to exotic locations is that they cost money. *Lots* of money. In fact, they really should consider offering coupons or something at the borders of coastal states. No such luck though.

So I concocted an ingenious plan.

The plan was that I would begin praying in September for a trip to Mexico next May . . . and that the trip would be *free*! I'm not kidding. I got on my knees every single day and asked God to fly us to a resort in Mexico sometime in May at no cost to us. God can do anything, right? And he wants us to pray specifically, right?

So I did.

Every day.

For months.

And I never told Ann about any of it. This was a special arrangement between God and me. The fall months turned into the holidays, but no free Mexico trip materialized. I kept praying. Thanksgiving. Christmas. New Year's Day.

Nothing.

So by the time January rolled around, I began to think that I better come up with another plan because it appeared that God was doing nothing on his side of our deal, even though I was still doing my part of begging him daily.

And then the miracle happened.

I had just walked off the stage after preaching on a Sunday morning when a young couple I had never met approached me. His name was Derek, and his fiancée's name was Tiffany. They were wondering if I might be available to officiate their upcoming wedding. I told them all about the premarital procedures at our church, and they replied that they would willingly go through the process, but that they actually needed an answer from me right now. When I asked why, I heard these precious words—words I will never forget.

"Well, our wedding is this May at an all-inclusive resort in Mexico," Derek said. "Tiffany and I will fly you and your wife down there free for a week if you can do our wedding."

Did you catch the *free* part?

Did you catch the *all-inclusive* part?

More importantly, did you catch the *free* part?

This was nothing short of a God-sized miracle. I jumped into Derek's arms and kissed him on the cheek, which wasn't weird at all. He had no idea that God had just answered months of prayers.

Ann and I had never been to an all-inclusive resort before. "All-inclusive" is Spanish for "tightwad's dream"—I'm no linguist, but I'm pretty sure that's right. Regardless, when you arrive at one of these resorts, they give you a little wristband that lets everyone know that from here on out, everything at the resort is completely and totally free for you to partake of to your heart's content. No charge for food. No charge for drinks. Nothing. It's all paid for with your registration fee—which, of course, was paid for by Derek and Tiffany.

Ann and I spent the first few days of our trip basking in the sun and fun of our all-inclusive Mexican wonderland. We were virtually oblivious to anyone else being on the grounds of our private little retreat. By the third day, I had almost completely forgotten about the upcoming wedding ceremony when we bumped into Derek and Tiffany. "Hey," they said, "we were hoping you guys might hang out with us and our wedding party a bit. We brought you down here to help us influence our friends who don't go to church. We figured you two would be a positive influence on them considering Jesus."

Now there's a concept: have a positive influence on people

considering Jesus through a wedding. Derek and Tiffany had some serious vision for their wedding, and it wasn't just to enjoy Mexico. We were in.

We asked what they were doing that evening, and they suggested we join them and their friends, who were meeting for dinner and one of the shows. We told them we would be there.

Ann and I showed up early and grabbed seats toward the front of the outdoor ballroom. There must have been more than one hundred dinner tables in front of the huge curtained stage. We had a very enjoyable dinner with the wedding party, and we were looking forward to the show.

Just before dinner ended, a worker from the resort asked Ann and me if we would like to volunteer to be in the show. He wouldn't tell us what we were volunteering for, but the next thing we knew, we were backstage with seven other couples.

As we waited, the curtain opened, and the emcee walked out onto the stage with a microphone. He then announced to the crowd that we were about to engage in a dance competition. "These eight couples will dance to different styles of music from around the world, and you will vote them off—one couple at a time. The last standing couple will win a grand prize."

At that moment all I could hear were crickets. Ann and I are the worst dancers ever. We love to dance. We even want to be good at dancing, but we simply are not. Well, Ann is a good dancer, but I'm terrible.

The music began with a rousing waltz: *1–2–3. 1–2–3*. It took only a few three-counts to demonstrate that we stunk at dancing. We kept awkwardly waltzing around the stage, just praying we would be the first team to be voted off. As always, our prayers were answered—we were indeed the first couple to be voted off by the audience.

Whew, am I ever glad that's over!

As we were walking back to our seats, the emcee asked us who we were and where we were from. I replied, "Dave and Ann Wilson from Michigan." I don't know if the crowd was filled with Midwesterners, but all of a sudden, the audience began cheering loudly for us to return to the competition. It was the only time in my life that I would have preferred a "boo!"

The emcee heard their collective request and said, "Dave and Ann, you are back in!"

"No, that's okay," I sheepishly replied. "We're fine sitting right here and watching. Really."

But he and the audience wouldn't have it—we were back in this competition whether we wanted to be or not . . . and for the record, it was "not."

Even so and against all conceivable odds, both earthly and heavenly, after five more songs we stood among the final three couples left dancing. *Yikes*. For these final three couples, the emcee informed the audience that we would now be dancing one couple at a time for the grand prize.

"Dave and Ann from Michigan, you are up first."

Of course we were. As we walked to the front of the stage, he revealed that the final category of music was "sixties music, acrobatic." I asked him what he meant by acrobatic, and he simply replied, "The more acrobatic you are, the better your chance of winning the grand prize."

What you need to know at this point is that I am extremely competitive. In fact, my desire to win proved in this instance to be even stronger than my disdain for being in this dance competition. Furthermore, no one is more competitive than I am—except, that is, my lovely wife, Ann. We both hate to lose, no matter what it is. (Perhaps now you see why we have so much to write about surviving arguments in marriage.)

Oh, and let's not forget that there was a little thing called "the grand prize" that the emcee kept mentioning. I figured this prize was probably another free trip back to this resort.

Did you catch the *free* part?

So we were *all in*!

If there is one more thing you should keep in mind about this whole scenario, it would be that Ann was a gymnast for most of her life. So when he said "acrobatic," my eyes lit up. I knew she was—and still is, by the way—more than capable of performing a vast array of gymnastic moves . . . aerials and roundoffs and such. My Ann can do more one-armed push-ups than I've ever even dreamed of attempting.

Just before the music started, I leaned over to her and whispered, "If you end this baby with a one-armed push-up, we win!" She looked back at me with that competitive glint in her eye and said, "Got it!"

The music started, and off we went—well, actually off *she* went. I quickly migrated to the back of the huge stage and proceeded to do my little dance moves—picture the awkward fusion of John Travolta in *Saturday Night Fever* with Kevin James in *Hitch*. I was waving my arms, shaking my booty, and doing a little "Q-tip" move while Ann was bringing the house down.

She gracefully darted back and forth across the stage, nailing a series of death-defying gymnastics stunts through the air. She landed each perfectly, and the crowd was going nuts! With all the oohs and aahs, it sounded as if people were watching a fireworks show rather than a dance competition. I just did my little dance moves at the back of the stage while whispering, "Go, girl, go!" It was obvious which one of us was the star.

As the music was coming to a close, we both instinctively knew we needed a grand finale. I moved to one end of the stage, while Ann had flipped her way to the other. As we locked eyes,

I impulsively came up with a stellar idea. I bent forward and made a motion for her to come jump through my arms to close this incredible dance sequence we (and I use the term *we* lightly) had just pulled off.

She responded with a look of confusion. So once again, I formed a circle with my arms and motioned for her to come and jump through it. Once again, she looked perplexed. I couldn't fathom what was so hard to understand about this! My arms were in a perfect circle, just like a hula hoop. In my mind, I was envisioning our own version of the show at Sea World, where Shamu the whale jumps out of the water through that huge hula hoop, perfectly executing his little flip back into the water at the end. In my visions of grandeur, I could visualize Ann leaping through my arms and landing this perfect flip—floating effortlessly and skillfully to the floor and finishing it all off with the aforementioned one-armed push-up as I came up behind her and dramatically spread my arms as if to say, "Ta-da!" The crowd would no doubt go crazy, probably even giving us a standing ovation.

And of course, at the time, there was not even one solitary reservation within me regarding the wisdom of comparing my wife of two and a half decades to Shamu the whale or of asking her to flail through the air toward certain death.

After all, there was a grand prize to be won.

Being the marriage experts we were, something in Ann finally clicked, and she signaled that she completely understood my Shamu fantasy and was more than ready (if not eager) to fling herself through the air like a huge oceangoing mammal. She began sprinting toward me—and I mean *sprinting*. Imagine the way they run toward the vault in the Olympics—and I was the human vault.

There was a look of determination in her eyes. *This is why*

I married this woman! Look at that look. She does nothing halfway! I could tell she was going all out to win the grand prize and another free trip back to this exotic resort. For a split second, all was right with the world.

As she approached me, she launched into the air with inconceivable height and skill, far above my hula hoop arms. I figured she had outleaped the plan, so I quickly moved out of her way to let her land unencumbered. It was still going to be an amazing ending, so I spun around and continued doing my own little jig for the finale—yes, I never even saw the landing!

But I did *hear* it.

The loud thud could be heard even above the blaring music. It sounded like someone had crashed hard to the ground—perhaps someone who had been expecting someone else to catch her. Yep, you guessed it. Somehow, Ann thought I was going to catch her in midair and spin her around like Patrick Swayze and Baby in *Dirty Dancing*. If there was ever an example of the differences in the way we think, this was it. She was thinking about Patrick Swayze; I was thinking about Shamu.

As she crashed to the stage, the audience let out a collective gasp. I didn't know if she was okay, but I knew that either way, I was a dead man. The thud must have resonated somewhere deep within me, because it jarred something loose in my cave-man brain. I suddenly understood what Ann had been thinking, and her logic now made perfect sense to me, as it would to any reasonable human. Why in the world would I have turned my back as she flew through the air? I just couldn't believe I had let her fall that hard.

When I turned around, Ann was lying facedown . . . and thankfully, she was laughing hysterically. I looked at the audience, and they looked back at me with sheer astonishment. It no doubt appeared to them that I had pulled away from the stunt as some sort of joke, like Lucy pulling the football away from Charlie Brown. In fact, I got scowls from people the next two days all around the resort because they couldn't believe I could be that unkind to my wife. I tried to explain, but they just rolled their eyes.

I helped Ann to her feet, and it was obvious she was in pain. The full extent of her injuries wasn't yet clear, but I was confident that what came next would make all the pain disappear in an instant: we won first place. In fact, the audience votes were unanimous. Perhaps they were sympathy votes, but we really didn't care because the grand prize was going to make it all worth the trouble.

So what was the grand prize? Brace yourself . . .

It was two T-shirts.

It got worse though. When we got back to Michigan and went to the doctor, we learned that Ann had broken both her wrists on that fateful fall to the stage. Yes, it was that bad—and I felt horrible.

But Ann? Not so much. Even as the doctor was putting the casts on her arms, she continued to laugh about the whole ordeal.

Giving 100 Percent

If there's one thing our two-parts-luxurious, one-part-disastrous tropical getaway revealed, it was that in this marriage, we're all in. Everyone who knows Ann knows that she is an "all in" kind of girl. She does nothing halfway—and I mean nothing. She is all in . . .

in her walk with God
as a wife to me

as a mom
at her work

There is nothing in her life where she gives merely 90 percent or even 95 percent. She is 100 percent all the time. This
is one of the main reasons I married her. She will do whatever
it takes to make anything she is involved in into something
memorable and spectacular.

Marriage is creatively designed to be an "all in" endeavor.
Anything less than this waters down the divine invitation to
share together in both adventure and adversity in ways "half
in" can never sustain. Many couples miss this key fact in the
beginning of their journeys together, which often leaves them
feeling either disillusioned or abandoned in the middle of their
life together.

But no matter where you are in marriage—not yet there,
at the beginning, or cruising along with years behind you—it's
never too late to discover the infinite value of being "all in" in
your marriage in the way God intended for you.

Give It All You've Got

Years ago, Ann and I adopted a life verse for us as a couple:
"Whatever you do, work heartily, as for the Lord and not
for men, knowing that from the Lord you will receive the
inheritance as your reward. You are serving the Lord Christ"
(Colossians 3:23–24 ESV).

"Whatever you do." Those are strong words. God could
have left it vague or merely specified a few areas of life. He could
have said, "When your husband is gentle and kind" or "When
your wife encourages you as a husband or father." But instead,
God blanketed all of our life with an invitation to see all of life

as what it really is: meaningful to him. Whether it seems trivial or not, it matters. It is a call to give it all we've got, all the time.

These words have comforted and corrected me so many times in marriage, mainly because it is so easy to miss the normal "whatever" moments. When the office has sucked the very life out of your soul. When you are sick or injured. When the kids are absolutely freaking out for no apparent reason. When the schedule is lying in ruins, and *routine* seems like some word out of a foreign language.

In those "whatever" moments, we often settle for mediocrity. But a healthy marriage begins with a healthy mind-set, with a determination that both of you—*all* of each of you—are all in for the same goal. And most importantly, you both are willing to fight for it more than you are willing to fight against each other.

Marriage is hard. Really hard. It's easy for us to begin with an "all in" attitude, but then when life turns tough (and it always will), we pull back, often expecting our spouse to step it up. And yes, there are times when one of us is weak and the other must stand strong and hold things together—that's just a part of the partnership of marriage.

I'm not talking about tough times in life's circumstances as much as I'm talking about tough times in the way each of you view your marriage itself. You may need to "tag out" at times so your spouse can clean up the latest mess the dog made in the living room. This is normal.

But when it comes to those moments when the marriage itself is facing extreme difficulty, too many couples "tag out" instead of going "all in" together. When you feel this in yourself, in order to survive and find your vertical perspective, you must actually forget your spouse, if just for a moment. Stop blaming them. Stop picking apart their faults to the exclusion of your own.

Yes, my friend, what about *you*? Is it time for *you* to step it up? To go all in. Or maybe to go back to being all in. Bringing your whole self to the table every single day.

Ann has taught me so much about this perspective—and believe me, it has been no cakewalk being married to me. I have let her down time after time as I have allowed my selfishness to dominate my actions. Instead of pursuing her and seeking to meet her needs, I have looked to see what she is doing for me. And yet, regardless of whether I deserve it or not, she keeps running toward me—over and over again throughout the years—with reckless abandon.

Yes, being "all in" in your marriage will sometimes leave you with serious injuries. Being brave enough to grow and to consistently reveal your real self to your spouse can sometimes be scarier than flying through the air on a little stage in Mexico. You might hurl yourself into the air emotionally, spiritually, or even romantically . . . only to discover that your spouse has failed to catch you—that's just reality.

And then when you are putting the pieces back together after a moment of disillusionment, argument, or the like, it is all too easy to vow to yourself, *I will never do that again! It hurt too bad!*

Ann knew that story all too well—both in our marriage and in her wrists. And yet, she took the leap anyway. Sometimes I have caught her; often I have not. But man, did we ever watch God put on a show in our marriage. I promise you this: God *has never* and *will never* drop you!

Our Safety Net

And there it is—the subject of the story changed (as it should) from "me and Ann" to "me, Ann, and Christ." When Christ is in the story and you respond to his vertical-first invitation, even painful moments (like having casts put on both your wrists) will be peppered with a sense of joy that is counterintuitive to your circumstances. This is the vertical variable. This is the safety net for both of you.

Going—or remaining—all in for your marriage does not come without real risk of pain or injury, but that's no reason not to grab each other's hands and dance with everything you've got! Because the bottom line is that when (not if) you fall—and even if that fall is harder than you ever imagined—there is a Healer present who promises to pick you both up, tend to your injuries, and set you back out on the dance floor again together.

The best marriages see the risks that come with leaping together, but then trust even more in the promises of the One who can catch or mend any outcome that arises.

What a great opportunity this is to go "all in" in your marriage by moving your perspective to a vertical plane! As I've done so many times in our marriage, get down on your knees right now and surrender your full self to Jesus—even if you have done so a thousand times before. And even if you do this alone. Just like the vastness of the sky, what resides above us in Jesus is immeasurable—you can never run out of his love for you. You can trust him enough to ask him to give you a new strength, a new perspective, and a new commitment to being all in with the one he has given you in marriage.

Remember, you can't control your spouse; you can only change yourself. Well, you can't even do that, but Jesus sure can.

I promise you that if you leap into the air today, God will catch you. Your spouse may not (just ask Ann), but *he* certainly will.

But you'll never know until you leap.

Seventeen

VICTORY THROUGH
Surrender

Well, here we are! We are nearing the end of our time together, and just like it is in all marriages, it's been a journey. We did not set out to write a book that would answer all the questions, solve all the problems, and remove all the mystery from marriage. We only hoped to point you to the vertical solution in Jesus that can be the foundation for achieving the marriage you've always dreamed of.

We instinctively think that if we could just try hard enough, talk long enough, work efficiently enough, manage our time well enough, or even pray long enough, then we could make our marriage work. Again, this thinking is rarely conscious, but it is often embedded in the way we approach relationships. God's intervention begins to feel like a helpful supplement to the process *we* are in charge of. In other words, we believe that if we are left to our own devices long enough and with just the right circumstances, we can make a pretty good marriage for ourselves.

Out of all the tips and insights we have shared, we hope that when you put this book down, you will have come to realize that God is not optional, supplemental, or even a helpful puzzle piece to a better marriage. No, God is the very table on which the puzzle rests. He is not a supplement; he is the strength itself.

Go to God First

Years ago, we took a canoeing trip with some friends. One of them dropped a very expensive pair of sunglasses in the extremely muddy water. But the water wasn't that deep, and we knew the approximate place where he had dropped them, so how hard could it be to retrieve them again, right?

We dove and searched for more than an hour—and we found nothing. The challenge seemed simpler than it was, as did the solution. Finally, someone had the idea that many of us would consider to be "childish" or "unnecessarily religious," as if God wouldn't care about something as insignificant as a pair of sunglasses. Even so, this one person asked God to help us find what was missing.

On the next dive, the glasses were found. Lesson noted: go to God first rather than last. Or perhaps better said, just invite God into the situation now and see what happens.

Marriage seems simple when you're dating and the waters are crystal clear with romance, attraction, and promises of lifelong love. But along the way, you will most definitely find yourselves scouring the riverbed in muddy conditions looking for lost things—things that seem like they should be easy to find, like kind words, sexual desire, conflict resolution, or just a simple agreement on how to do the family budget. Instinctively, you will want to think that you can just keep diving and that eventually you'll find what you're missing. Many marriages— Christian marriages included—drown in these conditions and under these assumptions.

We almost drowned in our efforts to find what was lost. Thankfully, we stopped and went vertical. We made a habit of asking Jesus to lead us to the very things we just couldn't find on our own. Yes, we still had to paddle and swim. Yes, we still had to communicate on hard subjects and apologize for repeated wrongs. But every time, Jesus was faithful to find what was lost in the mud and restore what was most valuable—and all because of his grace that invited us to believe that *only* he can sustain our marriage.

When Jesus said, "Apart from me you can do nothing" (John 15:5), we often apply his words only to our ability to pray consistently or minister in our churches effectively. Why do we do this? He couldn't have been clearer. "Apart from me you can do *nothing*." Nothing. Nada. Zilch. Nunca. Do you get the idea?

Let's say it like this: apart from God's daily intervention you can do *nothing* to help your marriage. So then, a vertical mindset shouldn't be the supplement to the tips, tricks, and strategies for growing a healthy marriage; it should be the main course.

And the great news is that it is very simple. It's about asking. Believing that *you* are not the centerpiece of the relationship and that not everything hinges on *your* ability to right the wrongs. Isn't that what you really want anyway? Relief from the feeling that it's all up to you, when you know deep down inside that you are not capable of everything that marriage entails?

Freedom in Christ is not some churchy catchphrase; it's a real thing. But freedom only comes through surrendering control to the One who is in control. If we continue to fight against the call to let Jesus have control of our lives and marriages, then we keep randomly grabbing the steering wheel while Jesus is driving—and we all know what kind of fender benders (or worse) such actions will produce.

You don't need a big marriage book or conference to save your marriage; you need a big God. Jesus resurrects dead and lost things—and especially marriages. It isn't hard for him to do it either; the hard part is usually whether or not we will release control enough to seek and accept his intervention. We struggle to let go of the argument to see how Jesus might lead us to resolution—the very resolution we long for the most. But yes, it may mean you "lose" your strongest point in the argument in order to "win" in your marriage. Ask yourself whether that fight you've been in for hours, months, or even years really feels like freedom, even if you're right. What do you have to lose by losing your own way?

Losing yourself means gaining God and his intervention.

Relationship Phases

Every marriage goes through predictable and recurring phases. If we're not careful, these phases can lead to disillusionment and a brick wall of negativity. In actuality, the results are up to us. These phases are not "one and done." Instead, if the marriage endures, these phases will recur over and over, and it's up to us to recognize them and learn how to deal with them.

Let's use the letters from the word *REDO* to describe the phases.

THE ROMANTIC PHASE

During the dating days, there's just this sizzle. This spark. This magic. We bring that magic into our marriage and call it the *honeymoon*. This is the stage where couples fall all over each other. They drool at the very sight of the other. They can't seem to keep their hands off each other in public. It can be embarrassing at times, but they don't seem to care. Dave remembers a time when Ann used to rub her hands through his hair. Of course, those days are gone—and so is Dave's hair!

This phase is so fun. There's this energy and passion . . . and the whole world feels different. Just recently, a single guy approached Dave after church and said, "I'm on a spiritual high that I haven't been on in years!" Dave replied, "Are you dating somebody new right now?"

The young man replied, "How did you know?"

THE EXCITED PHASE

But then you move to *E*, which is generally a very fun phase as well. You could call this the *excited* or the *expectant* phase. Either word will work. Excitement and expectations arise from the romantic phase. You think it will always be this way—that the sizzle and the magic you have for the other person will always be there. Many people get married during this phase, thinking that their feelings will always be at this peak.

They are convinced that they have found "the one" and that he or she will always love and respect them like no one else ever could. We don't verbalize these thoughts, but in this phase, we can't imagine ever being let down by or disappointed in our spouse. In fact, when others tell us that disappointment might be ahead, we conclude that no one has loved each other as much as we love each other. We are perfect for one another, and we will always feel this way.

Enter the next phase . . .

THE DISAPPOINTED PHASE

You never know when a couple will hit the disappointed phase, but it eventually happens to all of us. Dave officiated the wedding of a couple just two months ago, and they've already asked for help because they feel they made the biggest mistake of their lives.

Now that seems like a *very* short honeymoon, but it doesn't take very long for our expectations, which were impossible in the first place, to be sorely unmet. The feelings wane—and the conclusion is that the marriage is in crisis. Something must be wrong if feelings have changed. People miss the fact that feelings *always* change and that this doesn't have to be a moment to panic.

But we panic anyway. We think, *This isn't anything like I thought it would be.* You can't put a number on it—not three weeks, three months, three years, or fifteen years—but there arises a moment when you look at your spouse and you suddenly marvel that he or she is not who you thought they were.

She never stops talking! He's not romantic anymore! All he wants is sex! He doesn't even use silverware when he eats, for the love of all things good and holy!

This is a real stage in marriages. When you're in the disillusionment or the disappointment stage, this is how you feel. And this is where the wounding really begins. We say things and do things that we thought we would never say or do. Like the night Dave told Ann that he would rather be dead than married to her—that was a low moment of disillusionment. Every marriage will face a moment like this.

So as you move from romance to expectations to disappointment, you wonder what to do.

At that point you must choose one of two options . . .

THE "O" PHASE
Over

The O is like a fork in the road. First of all, it can stand for *over*. It's called divorce. It's called breaking up. It's called the relationship being over. *We're done. We're not moving on. I can't do this anymore. I can't stay married to you. You're not the one for me.*

When a marriage breaks up, it's painful and horrible. Not only are you and your spouse affected, but your kids are affected—and your legacies are affected. Divorce is like a death, even in those cases where you must do it to protect yourself.

In marriage, this O is always incredibly painful and tragic. It's the end of a dream, and dreams die hard.

But there is another option . . .

Overcome

Overcome is a biblical term from the book of Revelation (see, for example, 2:7, 11, 17, 26 NASB). God calls us overcomers as followers of Christ because we have been redeemed and equipped to overcome the evil one. We overcome the struggles of life through the grace and strength of Christ.

In fact, you can't overcome without Christ. Again, the reason is simple: your spouse will *never* fill you like you long to be filled. Only Christ can do that. And if you continually try to get what you think you deserve from your spouse, you'll never get it—he or she doesn't have it. You'll always live in letter *D*—you'll always be disillusioned; you'll always be disappointed.

But when you understand that you can overcome through Christ, something beautiful happens: you go back to *R* and begin afresh. You get a *REDO*. It's like a cycle. Romance comes flooding back into your relationship. No, it won't be just like those early days when you first started dating—it might be even better than that! Jesus is the King of redos; his grace resets us and places us back at the place we could never conjure on our own.

This cycle can even play out in the same day. We have had conversations in our kitchen that were just filled with hurt.

In our woundedness, we have had to rely on Christ so that we could overcome and go back to find our first love together. Only Christ can take you from being "over" to being "in love" again, all in the same year—or even in the same day. As we've tried to convince you, the vertical influence of Christ is not just some sermon illustration; it is a very present, genuine, and miraculous reality of God's active love toward his people.

You'll be blown away by what Christ can do with the bad things you bring to him in your marriage.

When we're wounded, we isolate ourselves emotionally. We want to stay there, but if we do, we create the potential of missing his divine redo. Instead, we've got to move on past the offense and the isolation, even if the conversations are difficult, and let him restart the process.

Victory Comes through Surrender

Victory and survival come through surrender. Unlike the wars we fight physically, if you want to win in your marriage, you surrender. You give up. This doesn't mean you give up and say it's over. It means you give up your own say and declare instead, "I can't do this! I need someone bigger than me to do it—and it's not my spouse."

After more than thirty years of marriage, we've realized that we desperately need Jesus to be our foundation. He can't just be someone we *say* is our foundation; he must *really be* the foundation. When we both find life in him, we are filled up. And when we both are filled up by God, we can then be givers, not takers, toward one another. And by the way, if your spouse won't surrender to God, then you do it. You can only control yourself. Ask God to work a miracle in your spouse. That's his job, not yours.

Here is what we've learned: when we are not filled by Jesus, we try to get from each other what only God can give us. We make our spouse our god, and all spouses make lousy gods. When our spouse disappoints us, we conclude that we have married the wrong person, and the endless search continues.

In his book *Sacred Marriage*, Gary Thomas speculates that maybe marriage was never intended by God to make us happy, but rather to make us holy, to be more like Jesus.* When Ann is disappointed in Dave, it forces her to go to God. Dave does the same when he is disappointed in Ann. And as we each cry out to God, we find that he begins to mold and shape us to be more like Christ.

One of the reasons you are so disappointed in your marriage could be that Jesus is drawing you to him. Yes, counseling may help. Yes, reading a good marriage book may help. Yes, going to a marriage retreat may help. But the only thing that can truly transform you and your marriage is surrendering yourself and your marriage to Jesus. Nothing else will even come close to changing you like Jesus will.

The apostle Paul wrote, "I want to *know* Christ" (Philippians 3:10, emphasis ours). He didn't say, "I want to know *about* Christ." No. He said he wanted to know Jesus intimately. His full statement went like this: "I want to know Christ—yes, to know the power of his resurrection and participation in his sufferings, becoming like him in his death."

Everybody wants to know the power of God in their lives. Who wouldn't want that? But Paul says that the only way we can truly know God's power is to also know his suffering. Pain is a gateway to power. Our pain often pushes us to Jesus.

---

* Gary Thomas, *Sacred Marriage: What If God Designed Marriage to Make Us Holy More Than to Make Us Happy*, rev. ed. (Grand Rapids: Zondervan, 2015), 9–13.

You are in a war, and you will be wounded, but even in this pain, God has provided a place of beauty for you and for your marriage.

The best thing you can do for your marriage is to surrender—and keep surrendering—to Jesus. Cling to Jesus, and let him bring *his* victory to your life and your marriage. Please hear this: the answer to your marriage is *not* found in knowing or meeting your spouse's needs for love and respect. The answer is solely found in surrendering to Jesus. He doesn't just come into our lives and make us a little bit better. Jesus didn't come to make bad people good; he came to make dead people alive.

He does the same thing with marriages. When you surrender your life and marriage to Jesus, he comes in and does a full makeover. Same address, but totally different house. He takes a marriage from . . .

Death to Life
Hopeless to Hopeful
Powerless to Powerful
Unforgiveness to Forgiveness
Fearful to Fearless
Joyless to Joyful . . .

We hope this book has helped you see that Christ, and *Christ alone*, is your answer. He wants to do a miracle in your life and in your marriage. If you choose to go vertical right now, he will begin to work his miraculous, life-changing, legacy-transforming power.

I love how the Bible puts it: "In everything you do, put God first, and he will direct you and crown your efforts with success" (Proverbs 3:6 TLB).

What are you waiting for? It's your day to start a new life, marriage, and legacy!

Pray this right now:

Father, I surrender all of me to you right now. I put you first from now on and choose to find my life, my happiness, in Jesus alone. Fill me with your Son, Jesus, in such a powerful way that I became the man/woman you created me to be. In the power and the character of the name of Jesus I pray. Amen.

ACKNOWLEDGMENTS

Being first-time authors means there are a ton of people responsible for this book becoming a reality! From the bottom of our hearts, we want to say thank you to . . .

Dennis and Barbara Rainey—you invited us to become speakers for FamilyLife almost thirty years ago and became our mentors. Thank you for pouring into us all these years. We just take what you give us and give it to others. I think that's called discipleship.

Bob Lepine—believe it or not, you were the first to say, "Go write *Vertical Marriage*, and write it now." You were the spark that ignited this book. Thanks for believing in us.

Denny and Scoob—you kindly offered up your house for a week so we could write there. Thank you. Hope we can do it again soon.

John Driver—you took tens of thousands of our words and edited them down into something that is actually sensible. Your skill and care are exceptional, and we are forever grateful.

Austin—what a joy to call you both son and literary agent. You are really, really good at your job! Having you as our agent was a highlight of this journey. Without you, this book would just be another dream idea, but you made the dream come true. Thank you. We love you so much.

Zondervan Team: David Morris, Tom Dean, Sandra Vander Zicht, Dirk Buursma, Robin Barnett—you are all such pros, and you walked us through this process so well. We always felt so loved and valued. Thank you for believing in us and getting us to the finish line (yeah, we know the real work is just beginning).

Kensington Church—our partnership in kingdom work with Steve and Paula, Mark and Callie, and the staff at Kensington has brought incredible joy and true mission and purpose to our lives. There is no one who hears God's voice and immediately obeys like the people of Kensington. We are not worthy of your love and affirmation. Thank you for trusting and following us for the last twenty-nine years. This book is our thank you to you.

Detroit Lions couples—over the past thirty-three seasons, we have been impacted by countless coaches, general managers, presidents, and staff, as well as players and their wives. These men and women have believed in us, followed us, and shaped us into who we are today. And every *Vertical Marriage* truth was first tried out on you!

Debbie—you have served us faithfully for close to thirty years with unending energy and commitment. We could not have written one word without you taking care of every detail of our lives. You make two unmanageable people manageable, and we can never thank you enough.

T2 and The Vertical First Board—every great marriage has a great community around them. You are our soul mates. Your friendship, accountability, helpful skill, and belief in us have made our Marriage and Family Ministry a reality. Thank you for your unwavering commitment to us. Without you, we would still just be talking about a book.

Michelle—a special shout-out for taking the time to read the full manuscript and make edits throughout. There was a needed comment in almost every chapter. Your friendship and commitment to us bring out the best in us. Thanks for loving Ann so well.

Dick and Toot (Ann's mom and dad)—your marriage of sixty-eight years has been an inspiration to us and everyone around you! You have truly lived out all aspects of your marriage vows, and especially, "in sickness and in health," during this leg of your marriage. Thanks for being some of our best friends and always believing in us.

Jesus—you saved us and then saved our marriage. Your grace to us is truly amazing. Thank you for giving us the way and the truth and the only life worth living. You and you alone are what Vertical is. Without you there is nothing, and with you there is everything. May you multiply your grace, truth, and hope to thousands through these words.

Going Vertical

QUESTIONS FOR COUPLES

Read a chapter and then crawl in bed and discuss . . . or maybe sit by the fire or on the deck or in your car in the parking lot. Who knows where this may lead—a prayer on the floorboard maybe?

CHAPTER 1: SIX WORDS THAT CHANGED EVERYTHING

1. In your marriage, when have you been hit with a "brick"—a challenge, reaction, or situation you never saw coming?
2. What kind of impact has this "brick" had on your relationship?
3. What were, or are, your expectations about:
   - your marriage?
   - your spouse?
4. Are there things about your marriage you wish you could share with your spouse? What keeps you from doing so? How about trying it right now. (Just listen and affirm. No comebacks. Then take it vertical—either alone or together.)

CHAPTER 2: "I'VE LOST MY FEELINGS FOR YOU"

1. On a scale of 1 to 10, rate your marriage. (Keep in mind that this number will continually be going up or down.)

Why did you rate it there? (You may wanna pray before you explain.)

2. How do you deal with disappointment in your relationship? Talk about that with your spouse, and why you handle it that way.
3. How have the pressures and responsibilities of career, life, or kids affected your marriage?

Chapter 3: A Surprise in the Honeymoon Suite

1. How does James 1:1–5 conflict with many of the expectations we tend to have about a life spent following God?
2. How would you feel if you believed that God has been asking you the same question he asked Ann: "Will you die for me and sacrifice your life so that I can make _____ the person I want them to be?" Explain.
3. Discuss or recount some trials you and your spouse have been through together or are going through now. Dave always says, "Trials will make you bitter or better—the choice is up to you."
4. Sit quietly with God and ask him if there's anything he wants to say to you.

Chapter 4: The Vertical Starts Here

1. Everyone says God first, then family, and job last. Ask your spouse or a close friend if you're living these out in that order.
2. What makes it hard for you to live in that order of priorities?
3. Are there any changes you can make in your life and schedule that will refine your priorities?
4. Pull out your calendar and make these happen:
   - Divert Daily—fifteen minutes with God/taaalk time with your spouse

- Withdraw Weekly—a day of rest/date night each week
- Abandon Annually—spiritual retreat/marriage retreat

CHAPTER 5: "COME BACK HERE AND FIGHT LIKE A MAN!"

1. How did your parents handle conflict? What went well? What went wrong?
2. What is your conflict style—Win, Yield, Withdraw, or Resolve? How has that been helpful or hurtful?
3. Discuss a recent conflict you had. What went well, and what went wrong? What changes can you put into place to help? (This is for you to change *you*—not your spouse!)

CHAPTER 6: WELCOME TO THE JUNGLE

1. Where does selfishness show up most in your marriage? (If you just thought of how selfish your spouse is, you just proved the point! Haha.)
2. If you were Satan, how would you destroy your marriage?
3. How can you fight Satan instead of your spouse?
4. Discuss some strategies to help you fight the enemy instead of fighting your spouse. Here are some examples:
   - Don't fight when hungry, tired, or stressed.
   - Avoid making accusatory statements, and don't use a critical tone.
   - Don't eye-roll.

CHAPTER 7: THE SHAPES OF WRATH

1. Ask your spouse or a good friend if they think you have an anger problem. What kinds of signs do they see? (Be careful how you phrase this. Don't use words like "you always" or "you never." Start with, "I feel like . . . or "it seems like . . .")

2. Take a good look at your angry outbursts. What is the first emotion you skipped?
3. What's the best thing your spouse can do when you're angry? (Ask them.)
4. What's the worst thing your spouse can do when you're angry?
5. Is there someone you need to forgive? (Don't forget about forgiving yourself. Start by asking God for help.)

Chapter 8: Just Zip It

1. Ask your spouse if there is an area where you're not hearing them. (Don't respond right away. Think about it and ask God how you can change, and then discuss it the next day.)
2. Instead of fixing your spouse's problems, ask them what it would look like for you to just listen. (Don't be surprised if they ask you to put down your phone or turn off the TV.)
3. Are you more of a truth-teller or a lover when it comes to speaking the truth in love? If you are a truth-teller, how can you be more loving? (I had to pray about it and sometimes have friends help me rephrase things before I talked to Dave.) If you are a lover, ask God for the courage to speak the truth in love and find an accountability partner who will hold you to it.

Chapter 9: Tear Down That Wall

1. Do you feel like you have any unresolved issues, or bricks, in your relationship? What are they, and why do you think they haven't been resolved?
2. Ask your spouse if he or she feels like there are any bricks or walls that are separating you.

3. What's a first step *you* can take to get rid of bricks? Hint:
   - Pray.
   - Give a soft answer.
   - Apologize if necessary.
   - Seek and grant forgiveness.
4. Ask your spouse what words and actions speak love and respect to them in the midst of conflict? (If you've used your words to belittle, harm, or berate your spouse, apologize and seek forgiveness. Put that pride away. To do this honors God. Make it a practice you do often. It tears down walls.)

CHAPTER 10: "ALL I HEAR IS, 'BOO!'"

1. Women, ask your husband if he feels like you cheer for him. Ask him to explain his answer.
2. Guys, tell your wife what words or actions communicate respect to you.
3. What words or actions communicate disrespect to you? (Women, start taking your thoughts captive and catch yourself when negative thoughts about your husband wreak havoc in your mind. To counter those negative thoughts, start a cheer journal. Start logging what your man does right and what you're grateful for about him. After you fill several pages, go on a date and read it to him. Catch your husband doing something good each day, and cheer him for it.)
4. Guys, share with your wife one area where you can use more cheering.

CHAPTER 11: WHAT EVERY WIFE LONGS FOR

1. Men, ask your wife if she feels like you cherish her. Ask her to explain her answer.
2. Women, tell your husband what words or actions communicate love to you.

3. What words or actions make you feel unloved?
4. What does Ephesians 5:25 teach us about the way Christ loves his bride? How can this apply to your marriage? (Men, women long to be pursued. Each day, put a reminder on your phone to pursue her. It could be a text, buying her a couple of roses, vacuuming the house, or even giving the kids a bath. This will be the greatest investment for your marriage, and it will reap great dividends. Don't give up if she doesn't respond right away. Sometimes it can take a while.)

Chapter 12: Sex in the Chapel

1. What were your expectations about sex before marriage?
2. How has married sex been different from what you thought it'd be?
3. What is the best part of your sex life—or if you're struggling right now, what was the best part?
4. What's one thing you can do to make your sex life better?

Chapter 13: Don't You Think about Sex All the Time?

This can be a difficult subject to discuss, but try to go there.

1. How does stress, a crazy calendar, or kids affect your sexual intimacy?
2. Ask your spouse what you can do to help him or her get "in the mood."
3. If you're arguing about frequency, ask your spouse why they want to have more sex—or perhaps why they want to have less sex.
4. What does nonsexual touch look like to you? Tell your spouse if and why it's necessary.
5. Ask your spouse if there are any heavy "bags" they are carrying and how you can help.

CHAPTER 14: DAVE'S NECK PROBLEM, PART 1

1. Have you had a time in your life or marriage when you felt incredibly insecure? Explain. In what way has that insecurity affected your marriage?
2. Why is knowing your personal identity important in your marriage?
3. What is the hardest thing in your marriage and in your life to trust God with? What keeps you from surrendering that area to him now? God is asking you, "Can you trust me with _____?" What's your answer? (Take our advice. Let him have it . . . now!)

CHAPTER 15: DAVE'S NECK PROBLEM, PART 2

It's time to have "the porn talk."

1. Is there any sexual temptation you're hiding from your spouse? Pray and ask God to prepare your spouse's heart and to guide you through this conversation. (Don't be discouraged if your confession is not met with applause from your spouse for telling them. This conversation did not go well at first for us. Remember that your heavenly Father is cheering you like crazy for bringing this into the light!)
2. If you're struggling in this area as a couple, find a godly couple you can share this with. Ask them for help and accountability.
3. If your spouse is struggling, ask what you can do to help. Begin by praying for him or her.
4. Every husband needs another guy and every wife needs another woman who can help them. Who is that for you? Make the call today.
5. Dave listed four ideas that can offer help to men or women. How can these ideas be applied to your life and marriage today?

CHAPTER 16: ALL IN

1. Have you ever had a time in your marriage when it felt like one or both of you weren't completely "all in"? What led you there? How did it feel?

   It's decision time. No matter how hard it has been or how badly you are struggling in your marriage right now, you don't stand a chance unless you are fully committed to going the distance. A new life and marriage starts right now. Don't put it off until tomorrow. Commit, or recommit, this very moment.

   Are you willing to go *all in*? Then tell your spouse and tell God. He will meet you right where you are and give you his power to carry out this commitment. But if you're not willing, at least take time to think about this: *What is keeping me from taking the leap?*

CHAPTER 17: VICTORY THROUGH SURRENDER

1. Which marriage phase—Romantic/Excited/Disappointed/ "O" (Over or Overcome)—do you find yourself in right now?
2. What step or steps can you take to bring back some romance and excitement into your marriage?
3. What are you waiting for? Let's do this—now!